BRITANNIA BRIGHT'S

BEWILDERMENT

WILDERNESS

OF

WESTMINSTER

A Political Poem
in Rhyming Couplets
by
CLIVE JAMES

With illustrations by MARC

JONATHAN CAPE
THIRTY BEDFORD SQUARE

D1556735

Britannia Bright's Bewilderment in the Wilderness of Westminster was first performed at the Institute of Contemporary Arts on the night of June 28th, 1976, under the auspices of the Poetry International Festival: the author narrated and Russell Davies supplied all the other voices.

All rights to recital, of the whole poem or any part, are strictly protected.

Some of the drawings appeared originally in the *New Statesman*.

FIRST PUBLISHED 1976
TEXT © 1976 BY CLIVE JAMES
ILLUSTRATIONS © 1976 BY MARK BOXER

JONATHAN CAPE LTD, 30 BEDFORD SQUARE,
LONDON W C I

James, Clive
Britannia Bright's Bewilderment in the
Wilderness of Westminster: a political poem
in rhyming couplets.
ISBN 0 224 01319 X
1. Title 2. Marc
821'.9'14 PR 6060.A/
English poetry
Political satire

PRINTED PHOTOLITHO IN GREAT BRITAIN BY
EBENEZER BAYLIS & SON LTD
THE TRINITY PRESS, WORCESTER, AND LONDON

to
Gianfranco Contini

Wise men will apply their remedies to vices, not to names; to the causes of evil which are permanent, not to the occasional organs by which they act, and the transitory modes in which they appear. Otherwise you will be wise historically, a fool in practice. Seldom have two ages the same fashions in their pretexts and the same modes of mischief. Wickedness is a little more inventive. Whilst you are discussing fashion, the fashion is gone by. The very same vice assumes a new body. The spirit transmigrates; and, far from losing its principle of life by the change of its appearance, it is renovated in its new organs with the fresh vigour of juvenile activity. It walks abroad, it continues its ravages; whilst you are gibbetting the carcass, or demolishing the tomb.

—BURKE

A GUIDE TO THE CHARACTERS OF THE WESTMINSTER WILDERNESS

BRITANNIA BRIGHT, a Girl Reporter.
BERT BRIGHT, her father: a jig-fold crimper.
BERYL BRIGHT, her mother.
ARIANNA SNAPITOPHOULOS, a Greek bombshell.
LORD BROWNALE, a Labour peer.
THE RIGHT HON. OLD MAC MCHACK, a well-loved
　ex-Prime Minister.
HEIDI HAYHOE, a friend to Britannia.
MIDGE MOLE, another friend to Britannia.
HAROLD INSIGHT, editor of the *Sunday Times*.
ENOCH EUNUCH, an Independent Voice.
JOHN PAUL GINGER, a provocative journalist.
NIKITA KIKITINSKI, a Soviet trade-union leader.
LEN MUMBLE ⎫
HUGHIE SCREWIE ⎬ three British trade-union leaders.
JACK JOKE ⎭
CLIVE PERKINS, a Welsh white-collar trade-union
　leader.
JOAN BRAKEBALL, a television interviewer.
QUINTIN SWINE, LORD HOGWASH, a Tory
　patriarch.
JERRY MERRY, leader of the Liberal Party.
CLEMENT DOGFOOD, a Liberal M.P.
'SIRLOIN' SMITH, four more Liberal M.P.s.
HOWARD HORRID, editor of the *New Statesman*.
JOHN GALLSTONE, a financial wizard.
SIR KEITH YOYO, a Tory ideologist.
BOB MCKEEN, a B.B.C. psephologist.
ROBIN BRAY, a B.B.C. front-man.
WILLY WHITEFISH, a Tory minister.
TED TEDE, a respected ex-Prime Minister: leader of
　the Tory Party.

MARGO HATBOX, another leader of the Tory Party.

WILHELM KAISER, editor of *Punch*.

ST MALCOLM MOTHERMILK, a holy man.

BRIEN BORON, a hack.

PAUL PHUTT, a radical journalist.

SIR MAX AXE, a Tory press lord.

LORD CHIFFCHAFF, a strategical thinker.

LORD PITPROP, a coal-man.

TARIQ EL FRIQ, a political agitator.

JIM CREED, a Scots Communist.

MAGNUS MASTERMIND, a B.B.C. front-man: later commander of the Icelandic gunboat *Thor*.

DAVID DROSS, a television personality.

TONY CROSSLINE, a Labour philosopher.

ROY JUNKET, a man of conscience: Home Secretary.

MICHAEL PHUTT, uncle to Paul: a Left-wing theorist.

TONY WEDGTAIL TITT, a scourge of the privileged classes.

JOKIN' JIM and DISMAL DENIS, a double act.

RAVEN REDRAG, actor and radical.

VICTROLA REDRAG, actress and radical: his sister.

HAROLD WILES, leader of the Labour Party and Prime Minister of Britain.

PETER JAW, the Cleverest Young Man in England.

MARY WILES, wife to Harold: a poet.

LORD TEDDYBEAR, the Poet Laureate.

PEREGRINE PRYKKE, a critic.

LADY FREESIA FRUITCAKE, a biographer.

JOE GORMLESS
ARTHUR NUMSCULL } three more trade-union leaders.
SID GHREASE

JOHN PRODLOW
DAVID SLEET } the remaining Liberal M.P.s.

SIR ANCIENT STATELY-HOME, ex-Prime Minister: a listed building.

AIRY WAVE and AGNES MAUDE, two Tory hard-liners.

MICHAEL MUSCLETONE, a hustler.

RHOLLS ROYSON, a Black Paper diehard.

REGGIE MUDLING, a prodigal son.

LORD ECCLESCAKE, a dunce.

ST JOHN STILTHEELS, an exotic.

LORD BOOBY, an after-dinner speaker.

WYATT TWERP, an eccentric.

NIGEL DAMPSTAIN, a gossip.

RICHARD INKWELL, editor of *Private Eye*: a
credit to the school.

BRON WAN, a would-be wit.

JOHN BRAINWAVE
BERNARD BEAVER } the Bertorelli Blackshirts.
KINGSLEY KONG

VERE HAMSTRUNG and RUPERT MUDRAKE, two
press-proprietors.

WILLIAM DENS-FOGG, editor of *The Times*: an owl.

LADY HIGHRISE OF THE TOWERS, a fashionable
hostess.

SIR RICHARD SWAMP,   chairman of British Rail.

NIGEL NYLON, editor of *News at Ten*.

WEE GEORGIE (later LORD) WIDE, chairman of
Tightenbelt and Buckledown, publishers.

CLAY CROSS, a comedian.

THE SHREWSBURY TWO, a pop group.

ERIC EFFING, a Labour organizer.

ROBERT MULISH, Government Chief Whip.

RAY GRUNTER, a heavy.

MICK THE KARD, a bookie.

LORD COWCUD, erstwhile editor of the *Mirror*.

WILLY HECKLETHRONE, a Republican.

SIR MANNY CHINWAG, a garrulous old fool.

SHIRLEY WHIRLEY, a treasure.

ROY RATTLESNAKE, a coming boy.

BABS BUSTLE, a Labour matriarch.

HENRY KISSINGER, a modern Metternich: saviour
of Cyprus.

KEN TROTT and KIKA KLUTZ, two Strolling
Revolutionary Players.

CHARLES CHARMING, PRINCE OF WALES, heir
  to the Throne.
PRINCESS ANNE, a centaur.
HAROLD HALF-PINT, an elliptical playwright.
SIR HUGE WELSHMAN, communicator (ret.).
CHIEF CLERK, an aesthete.
LORD FATMAN, a sage.
LORD BUTCHFIELD, a photographer.
LORD POLAROID, a tragedian.
LORD WIGGLE, a racecourse official.
SIR RICHARD JIGGLE, leader of the Bleeding Gits:
  a pop idol.
DR FRINGE ('Jonathan'), a prodigy.
RUSS KENNEL, a controversial film-director.
HARRY SEASLUG, a rotund tenor.
PETER BALLS, a controversial man of the theatre.
JOE STRANGE ⎫
BERNARD DONFORHIRE ⎪
LADY FARKINELL ⎬ attendants on Harold
TOMMI BUDA ⎪ Wiles
NIKKI PEST ⎪
GERALD MAUFFPIECE ⎭
HER MAJESTY QUEEN ELIZABETH II

AND

St Ignatius Loyola, Olga Korbut, Sir Thomas
Malory, Pabst, Lloyd George, Palmerston, Cardinal
Manning, Oliver Cromwell, George Canning, William
Cobbett, Brunel, Flaubert, Jean-Claude Killy,
Beethoven, Alexander of Macedon, the Douanier
Rousseau, Kokoschka, Turner, Whistler, Monet,
Queen Elizabeth I, Asquith, Sir John Simon,
Nietzsche, Hitler, Kierkegaard, Mother Teresa,
Lord Chesterfield, Byron, the Shah of Iran, Aneurin
Bevan, Marconi, Karl Marx, Trotsky, Edith Cavell,
Jackie Charlton, Casanova, Charles de Gaulle, Corot,
R. H. S. Crossman, Barbra Streisand, Charles
Bronson and many more.

BOOK ONE

O F POLITICS I sing, both Left and Right,
And of the sprightly scribe BRITANNIA
BRIGHT,
To *Albion* the dearest of all daughters
And pipkin of Political Reporters.
Britannia! A cognomen which to fit
The metre I shall doubtless shrink to *Britt* —
Which is, for all the appellation galls her,
The name that almost everybody calls her.
Britt Bright. A new *Flick Fark*, you ask? You needn't.
No cipher like her nitwit antecedent,
Britannia Bright's a brilliant representative
Of what one might (and here if I sound tentative
It's out of circumspection, not self-doubt)
Say *British* Education's All About —
The never-ceasing nurturing and nourishing
And fretful fussing-with until they're flourishing
Of high *I.Q.*'s drawn out to Full Potential
By being fed with everything essential
(Or vaguely thought appropriate) for both
Their Spiritual and Intellectual GROWTH,
At costs which a self-sacrificing Nation
Might not recover for a generation.
In *Britt Bright*'s case, however, the return
On outlay was as high as you can earn
Without receiving *gratis* and tax free
A really juicy slice of the *North Sea*,
Since for the price of paste, paints, pens and pencils
Plus sundry other scholarly utensils
This lucky land was privileged to acquire
A citizen prepared (prepared? On fire!)
To further the best interests of Society
According to her gifts and its variety,

(13)

To draw conclusions and to make connections
And cast her vote with forethought in Elections.
The raw ore of her mind refined and milled
Without a single spark of fine steel spilled—
The fine steel forged and tempered, checked and
   weighed
And ground and filed and honed into a blade—
Britt grew up as a living testament
To how our crushing taxes might be spent
On something in the long run far less frangible
(Because so much more solid, if less tangible)
Than supersonic aircraft no one wants
Produced at vast expense to small response—
For surely it counts more to train a brain
Than transmit businessmen to bleak *Bahrain,*
Where even if they should arrive still well
The plane they came on's all they've got to sell.
But *Britain*'s Future is too vexed a question
At this stage for mellifluous digestion.
To force that spiky subject down your throat
You'd need to be an ostrich, shark or goat.
I'd sooner focus on *Britannia*'s Past
And treat the grim stuff later on, or last,
Or never. Let no overtones obtrude
Of Doom. Let talk of Chaos be eschewed.
Let tattle of Inexorable Forces
Or hoofbeats of *Apocalyptic* horses
Be paid no heed. Let this, let that, let not ...
Let what? You say let up? Oops. I forgot.
I'd meant to keep the tone from sounding leaden
And here, by banning chat of *Armageddon,*
I've merely served to concentrate attention
On what we're all determined not to mention.
But to resume. *Britannia*'s school career,
Though glittering, need not detain us here.
It matched that of my hero *Perry Prykke*
Without so much about it to dislike,
Since *Perry*'s urge to spell words and do sums
Was really much less his than his mad *Mum*'s,

While from the very start *Britt*'s thirst for Learning
Reflected a deep-seated Inner Yearning.
She studied hard because she had her heart in it.
Parental pressure plainly played no part in it.
How could it have? For *Britt Bright*'s wholesome folks
Were really so fair-minded they were jokes.
They did their best to see that nothing thwarted her,
But didn't push the girl—merely supported her.
A pair of paragons I should be proud
To sing the praises of if time allowed—
A perfect partnership I should leave littered
With wild encomiums if time permitted—
The *Brights* from their abode in *Cricklewood*
Looked out on *Britain* and they found it good.
A foreman in a factory that crimped folds
In metal jigs for dies that stamped out moulds,
Britt's DAD worked hard

> ('Worked hard? I bloody slaved.')

And everything he earned his good wife saved,
Except for what she spent on *objets d'art*
Which crammed the house like humbugs in a jar—
The *Bright* ménage was lined with tiers of shelves
Abounding with glass tigers, fawns and elves,
While china geese flew up the parlour wall
And similar ceramics shared the hall
With copper trumpets, chiming brass barometers
And counterweighted cuckoo-clock thermometers.
Says *Mr Bright* today:

> 'Your *Welfare State*

Was ruined by your *Common Market*, mate.
One time they spent your tax like it was meant.
I'm glad *Britt* came along before that went.
Your stamp in them days bought things you could *see*.
The Country's had it now, if you ask me.'
'The Country's had it now,'

> his wife concurs.

'Whatever that girl wanted, it was hers.
In them days you got something for your stamp.
The Council came to fix your rising damp.

(15)

Your *Common Market*, that's what ruined that—
And now there's your Inflation and your *VAT*.'
Let this staunch dialogue be proof enough
That *Britt Bright*'s Background was good solid stuff.
The *Brights* were dull, dependable and nice:
Whatever went for him, for her went twice.
Their child obeyed, respected and adored them
And, as was unavoidable, outsoared them—
So so must we. Let speed be of the essence
Recounting how from pre- through post-pubescence,
From Comprehensive school to ivied Cloister,
The world of self-improvement was *Britt*'s oyster—
A bivalve mollusc aching to be cracked,
Hacked, smacked, whacked, sacked and generally
   attacked.
Strike up the Motley, then. On with the Revels.
The *Devil* take all drivel of A-levels,
Of Places, Preferences and Interviews—
Suffice to say *Britannia* couldn't lose.
She had the looks, the brains *and* the vitality:
Assessing her was merely a formality,
Which being done, the avalanche was on—
The Varsities went ape for her *nem con.*
The letters of acceptance fell like hail.
Some mail was sent by rail and some by sail
And some across the desert by safari.
For *Brett* to be in *statu pupillari*
Seemed suddenly the principal condition
For Institutes of Tertiary Tuition
To go on with the struggle for existence;
Their importunities verged on insistence.
But how to choose? To please her *Mum* and *Dad*
She plumped for what she knew would make them glad.
Which doesn't mean that either was a snob—
They just thought it the best place for the job.
And so *Britt* went to OXFORD. I won't dwell
On all the *mise en scène* you know so well,
The ashlared walls of friable blonde stone
As soft to look at as an ice-cream cone,

The pale blue sun-dials, rusty lightning rods,
The tufts of buttercups in green baize quads,
The dreaming river-light, the dreaming heat,
The dreaming dons colliding in the street,
The scoop of melting snow cupped in the crocus—
And all that out-of-focus hocus-pocus.
Enough to note *Britt Bright* of *Somerville*
At once got down to business with a will.
As term succeeded term she sank her roots,
Sucked in the nutriment and put out shoots.
In *P.P.E.* she scored a string of Firsts
Despite the fact she only worked in bursts.
Preoccupied with *OUDS* or else with '*Isis*'
She dashed about in one perpetual crisis.
As always, an embarrassment of choices—
A coaxing babble of persuasive voices—
Beleaguered her. Her looks required a stage;
Her verbal aptitude, the printed page;
Her taste for Politics some kind of platform.
Should her career take *this* form or else *that* form?
Propelled by pluralistic predilections
Our girl was going off in all directions,
Until, like *Cinders* meeting the Good Fairy,
She bumped into a Student Luminary
Who seemed to have Life's problems well in hand,
With all that she surveyed hers to command.
It happened at an *Eights Week* cocktail bash
Thrown strictly for the Quality—no trash.
The *University*'s most stunning resident,
The *Union*'s first and foremost female *President*,
Britt's new-found friend was tall and well endowed
And everything she said was very loud,
As if delivered by a hill-top oracle
To someone bobbing off-shore in a coracle.
Put in your ear-plugs. Cover up your eyes,
For so much pulchritude can paralyse;
The system quavers at such oomph and bounce.
Sit tight and hold your heads while I announce
That most praetorian and least plebeian

Of Jet-Age *Junos* from the blue *Aegean*—
Though some say *Greece*'s gain was *Oxford*'s loss—
Yes, ARIANNA SNAPITOPHOULOS!
'I hear about you, *Bratt*,'

                  yelled *Arianna*,

The words erupting like a vast hosannah.
'So far you 'aven' got it all together
But one day you an' me birds of a feather.'
The *Grecian* demi-goddess bulked so large
One's nose got caught in her *décolletage*,
A wall of talcum like the Cliffs of *Dover*.
The scent of jasmine almost bowled *Britt* over.
'You ought to make the *Union* your arena.
You got the brains, the bones an' the demeanour.'
And here she smiled a smile so orchidaceous
It would have burned the pants off *St Ignatius*.
'Real soon you could be *Presiden'*, like me.
You even got my Femininity.'
While Arianna stood like a colossus
Transplanted rather carelessly from *Knossos*,
Britt drifted dazed around that laughing lawn,
Anticipation in her eyes like dawn.
The *Oxford Union*! O *sanctum sanctorum*!
For Free Men the supreme informal Forum!
The *Presidency*! O exalted seat!
Entrée to the Political *élite*!
While chimes of evening sounded from *Tom Tower*
Britannia licked her lips and tasted Power.
It tasted sweet. It always does, they say.
And off she went to dance the night away.

BOOK TWO

BETWEEN *Britt* and her newly chosen goal
There lay a more than slightly greasy pole,
Which normally takes several terms to climb.
But let's assume, to save ourselves some time,
That *Britt* attained the *Presidential* chair
The same way something flying through the air
So fast unaided eyesight can't absorb it
Abruptly stands revealed as *Olga Korbut*.
Lights, fanfares, drums, applause and ... disillusion.
Though perquisites were hers in great profusion —
The final weekly progress to the throne,
The fun of sitting high up and alone,
The thrill of being ogled from the gallery
While dolled up like a damsel out of *Malory* —
Britt Bright was soon obliged to face the fact
The Golden Bowl in one respect was cracked:
The Politicians willing to Debate
In every case were wildly out of date —
The elbows keen to lean on the despatch box
Unfailingly were frailer than a matchbox.
'Dear *Diary*,'
          wrote *Britt*,
                    'My hat! I mean
It's utterly a geriatric scene!
They're dropping in their tracks! *Christ*, what a crew!
For *this* I changed my accent in the loo?'
Where common people go to move their bowels
Britt Bright had gone to purify her vowels
Until she could approximate the sound
For which TV's JOAN BRAKEBALL is renowned.
Those awkward diphthongs painlessly deleted
While Madam remains comfortably seated!
We rid you of the consonant that rankles

(19)

While you relax with knickers round your ankles!
But hold it. No commercials. Back to *Britt*,
Whose famous Journals seem composed to fit
My verse-form as if ordered in advance —
And yet I swear it's nothing more than chance.
Her pert prose just comes out as near as damn it as
Impeccably iambic rhymed pentameters.
'They mumble,'
                    Britt went on,
                                        'some kind of code.
They smell like cats run over on the road.
Their sinister D.J.'s are double-breasted.
Their shirt-fronts look like somewhere puffins nested,
And those revolting off-white bits of stuff
That poke out at the wrist you think are cuff
Are much more probably embalming cloth.
And every time they yawn, out pops a moth.'
Thuswise *Britannia*'s Presidential term
Was spent on entertaining the Infirm.
All known varieties of clapped-out speaker
Arrived week after week, weaker and weaker.
They always answered Yes to invitations
The Powerful regarded as vexations,
For though the Men Who Mattered wouldn't play,
The men who didn't wouldn't stay away.
Reflecting the sad truth that dereliction
Has ever given rise to florid diction,
They thought it no more pointless to make speeches
Than horses without riders to jump *Becher*'s,
And filibustered on without compunction —
Fulfilling faithfully their lack of function.
Britt's valedictory Debate, however,
Reflected her Committee's grim endeavour
To come up with a few Decision Makers
Who looked a little less like undertakers —
Some big-wigs, whether *Labour* or *Conservative*,
Who didn't smell of medical preservative.
A leading light from each major persuasion
Had graciously turned up for the occasion.

(20)

To hear LORD BROWNALE and OLD MAC MCHACK
The chamber was jam-packed from front to back.
To hear these stars of their respective teams
The place burst at the seams from floor to beams.
To hear such mighty Statesmen pit their wits
The students' hunger was as keen as *Britt*'s,
Who'd never looked more radiantly eager —
A fact which pleased *McHack*, the old intriguer.
He focused his attention during dinner
So tightly on her it was almost in her,
And while he set the table in a roar
With hoary tales of *Tory* days of yore
He ventured underneath it with a hand
Which unlike his lamented prostate gland
Was still intact and very keen for action.
For *Brownale*, though, the centre of attraction —
On which he lavished smiles, enticing banter
And, lastly, words of love — was the Decanter.
He cuddled and caressed its crystal stopper
In ways *Britannia* would have thought improper
Except she knew the fist that gripped the glass
Still skinned its knuckles for the Working Class —
In battle unremittingly embroiled
This gifted son of toil remained unspoiled.
Like fighting generals taking charge of trenches
Britt's two guests occupied their different benches.
Some fledgling orator proposed a Motion
Of whose import I don't retain a notion.
Another tyro rose up in rebuttal
And lost the thread attempting to be subtle.
A third was exquisitely soporific.
The total tedium was beatific.
Proponents and opponents fell and rose
Proposing to oppose and re-propose
While *Mac McHack* pretended deep enjoyment
And *Brownale* offered regular employment
To some exotic breed of silver flask
Not really that much smaller than a cask.
Eventually, when decades had elapsed

(21)

No faster than an epic filmed by *Pabst*,
The time arrived for *Brownale* to Support
The Motion. He rose up. If *Britt* had thought
The peer would show some hint of having dined
A trifle too well, she now changed her mind.
His speech, instead of being slightly slurred,
Was quite the most remarkable she'd heard —
For *Brownale*, far from being a bit drunk,
Was blotto. Blind pissed. Drunker than a skunk.
'Brothers and sisters, I came here tonight
By train and taxi. It just wasn't right.

Why couldn't you lay on a chauffeured car?
You just don't seem to grasp what manners are,
You youngsters of today. Also the wine
You might have made a *Latour '49*
Or else a *Mouton Rothschild*. Please don't think
I give a Continental what I drink —
As long as the stuff's booze then it suits me —
But I'm a man of standing, as you see.'
At which point he fell down. Thus the exordium
Lord Brownale gave the startled auditorium.
His peroration, based on the same format,
Was spoken while he lay flat like a doormat.
'The bastard tricked me! Me, his leading helper!
He fixed it so I couldn't win in *Belper*!
The *House of Lords* was just somewhere they shoved me
Because it scared them how the people loved me!
Oh *Christ*! Pink elephants with baseball bats!
They're after me! *Here come the purple rats*!'
Lord Brownale flailed about and drummed his heels
While shouting accusations and appeals.
At last he rolled beneath his bench and wept.
His sobs gave way to sniffs. To sighs. He slept.
Britt knew she should say something, but not what.
The pin-point of her beauty-spot felt hot.
Her lower lip displayed a tiny tremor.
It was *McHack* cut short her cruel dilemma:
His fingers all a-fidget where they gripped
A much unfolded and re-folded script,
With pouts and tics and twittering and pottering
Unheralded he bravely came forth tottering,
And instantly the *House*'s heart was his —
Which stunned him not at all. It always is.
'Dear Boys and Girls,'
                 began *McHack*,
                            'We live
In dark times. Mwaargh. I think you will forgive
My saying that the claws of a disease
Are burning us with poison till we freeze,
As if a panther wolfed us in its gorge.

(24)

Not only did my mother know *Lloyd George*
But I did too, and he once told me this—
Just stick to one idea the plebs can't miss
And deck it out with jokes and the odd pause.
And so I say that Socialism's claws
Will suffocate us all with their infection
Unless my Party wins the next Election.
A Wind of Change is what we'll bring about
If you'll just put us in and *Attlee* out.'
The notes *McHack*'s cold fingers fought to hold
Must be, *Britt* thought, at least two decades old.
His merest *mot* a hundred times re-hashed,
He burbled suavely onwards unabashed.
'As *Palmerston* once told me, "*Mac*, my lad,
You've Had It Good and. Mwaargh. That can't be bad."
A frigh'f'ly 'ficient man. Knew him quite well.
Got on with *Gladstone* better, truth to tell.'
And so he flannelled on, chock-full of charm,
But at a length which filled *Britt* with alarm.
'I well remember once *Cardinal Manning*
Invited me to dine. Or was it *Canning*?
Most likely it was *Cromwell*. My old pal.
The subject? *Suez*. Some kind of canal
Had been proposed to link the Hemispheres.
Of course *I'd*. Mwaargh. Supported this for years ... '
He'd hit his form. When midnight rolled around
Old Mac McHack still stoutly stood his ground.
He stirred up, with a giggle and a glance,
No end of anecdotal song and dance.
He kept up, with a wet wink and a snuffle,
A muffled but unruffled soft-shoe shuffle.
He clocked up, with much teetering and tittering,
Some pretty indefatigable wittering.
On tip-toe—for they did not want to hurt him—
The students began sadly to desert him,
Until at last, struck dumb with fear and pity,
There only remained *Britt* and her Committee.
Then finally her colleagues, too, departed—
Which left *Britt*, still enthroned but broken-hearted,

(25)

To wonder just how long he'd ramble on.
Another hour and even she was gone.
With age-old echo-shadows of the dead
Reverberating round his haunted head,
This lonely sage recounted great events —
An empty room the only audience,
Since *Brownale*, where he silently lay curled,
Was lost to view and dead to all the world.

BOOK THREE

'**D**EAR *Diary*,'
               wrote *Britt* as the fast train
Ran *East* to *London*.
                '*Jesus*, what a pain!
The whole thing was unutterably squalid.
Those two crocks cooled my big night good and solid.
We had to gag *McHack* with a wet rag
And send home *Brownale* in a plastic bag.'
Ignored by *Britt* the Valley of the *Thames*
Unfolded as she fashioned apophthegms.
Towards the city *Cobbett* called a canker
Our Heroine went speeding spilling rancour.
But well before the wheels ceased to revolve
Her bitterness had turned into resolve.
Britt's course of action somewhere between *Reading*
And *Paddington* set off on a new heading.
'Some day I'll have to choose what side to take,'
She wrote,
           'But choosing too soon's a mistake.
I won't seek Power. I'll seek to understand it
And turn my gaze where Truth seems to demand it.
To be a budding female Politician
Now seems to me a meaningless ambition.
Though I am forced to live on bread and water,
I shall be a Political Reporter.'
She closed her book as under *Brunel*'s vault
With squeaks and jolts the train came to a halt.
A tinny tannoy high up in the station
Said:
       'We regret that owing to Inflation
All passengers from *Oxford* except those
With heart-shaped yellow freckles on their nose
Must pay a one-Pound surcharge at the gate

For being only fifty minutes late.'
Without repudiating for a second
Her parents' way of life, *Britannia* reckoned
That nearer to the centre of the city
Was where she would confront the nitty-gritty,
And being in these matters very thorough
Soon found a bolt-hole in the *Royal Borough* —
A stretch of country which, rich in the *South*
And in the *North* extremely hand-to-mouth,
Encapsulates the Capitalist riddle.
Britt's new address was slap bang in the middle —
A dinky but desirable abode
High up in an old house in *Melbury Rd.*
In *London*, as you all know from TV,
Girls occupy a flat in groups of three.
Like *Kensington* itself, *Britt*'s new-found friends
Exemplified the two opposing ends
Of what one (granting one were ill-advised)
Might call the Spectrum. They were Polarized.
Their names were HEIDI HAYHOE and MIDGE MOLE.
Sweet HEIDI was a merry sort of soul,
An Upper Middle Class but never bumptious
Long-straight-blonde-haired-long-legged-simply-
   scrumptious
Unthinking product of that *status quo*
To which *Midge* was an unrelenting foe —
For *Midge*, although like *Heidi* bourgeois-born,
Was energized by Radicalized scorn.
She kicked Male Chauvinism where it hurt
And ground The System's nose in its own dirt.
A rabid proselyte for Women's Lib
She read not just '*Bananas*' but '*Spare Rib*'.
One tall and sweet, the other sour and squat,
What *Heidi Hayhoe* was, *Midge Mole* was not.
But both of them made *Britt Bright* feel at home,
And very soon on bathroom rails of chrome
Appeared *Britt*'s share of tights and no-bra bras,
And on the green glass shelves her range of jars,
Combs, bottles, curlers, boxes, aerosols

(28)

And suchlike bibelots and folderols.
But here I quell the fetishist compulsion
To itemize each lotion and emulsion,
Each carelessly creased item of apparel
That crammed the place like buck-shot in a barrel.
I simply say in my embarrassed mumble
The trio's pad was an enchanting jumble
Of all the ladylike paraphernalia —
The whole lace-panelled, scalloped-edged regalia —
Which some men find it quietly arousing
To spend an hour amongst discreetly browsing,
As *Flaubert* went through ladies' reticules
And held the contents to the light like jewels.
I simply say ... what am I simply saying?
I simply think my wits are simply straying.
To find such frills and fripperies delectable
At my age is no longer quite respectable.
But there you go. Before I start to sob
With shame I'll send *Britt* out to find a job.
A pre-cast palace of the modern sort
Half-way between a hotel and a fort
In *Grays Inn Road* is even for the cynical
Among aspiring journalists the pinnacle.
I mean the *Sunday Times*, whose marshalled forces
Of In-Depth News-Interpreting Resources
Forever drumming up some bold Indictment
Are always in a state of high excitement —
Though in their paroxysms of indicting
They don't come up with much exciting *writing*.
(Sour grapes. Their ad-rich rag could not be fatter
So if their prose is flat that's no great matter.)
Like shackled rowers powering triremes
The *Sunday Times* factotums work in Teams,
And left alone they're often at a loss —
That's everyone, of course, except the Boss,
The very touchstone of whose personality
Is charismatic Individuality.
Yes, HAROLD INSIGHT is the kind of man
You can't quite credit even when you can.

Compact, dynamic, eloquent and capable,
His vivid omnipresence inescapable,
He is as turbulent a human being
As ever took to editing. Or skiing—
An avocation he pursues with passion.
He hurls himself down *Alps* in daring fashion
And plugs the pricy pastime to his readers
In photo-features, articles and leaders.
Unconscious of all this, *Britannia* walked
Through *Insight*'s office-door, gaped, gulped and
    gawked.
The man behind the desk was wearing goggles.
His anorak had lots of zips and toggles.
'I'd heard you brought *McHack* back from the dead,
And now I see how,'
                    Harold Insight said.
'I *love* your stuff.'
                    He waved a dossier.
'I'll give you an assignment straight away.
We need an ENOCH EUNUCH interview.
He's living in a hot-house down at *Kew*.
Just start him up and catch his general drift.
All set to go? I'll show you to the lift.'
When *Insight* stood, *Britt* trembled at the knees.
He not only wore ski-clothes, he wore skis!
His thick-gloved hands picked up a pair of poles
And with his goggled eyes aglow like coals
He lurched across the Stippled *Wilton* floor
And paralleled into the corridor,
Down which he *schüssed* with piercing cries of
                                    '*Piste!*'
Erupting from him as his speed increased,
Until at last he yodelled,
                    'Look at this!'
And through his clenched teeth mimicking the hiss
Of injured snow he vaulted to a halt,
The slalom course complete without a fault.
And that was how *Britt* came to venerate
The *Jean-Claude Killy* of the *Fourth Estate*.

But now there was a change of atmospherics
So rapid that *Britt* would have had hysterics
If she had not instead been rendered dumb —
The speed of the transition left her numb.
From *Insight*'s ambience of snow and ice
By chauffeured car *Britt* transferred in a trice
To *Enoch Eunuch*'s world of humid fumes,
His glass and iron rooms of tumid blooms —
A mish-mash of botanical exotica
All tangled up and writhing like erotica
To form a fitting background for a specimen
Acknowledged by both larger men and lesser men

As worthy of respect, if not affection—
A rarity well meriting protection.
To this end the glass house had been constructed
Through which its famous tenant now conducted
The sweating *Britt Bright* at a stately pace,
Though he himself displayed upon his face
No hint of perspiration. Was his skin
Composed of wax lit coldly from within?
Inert and lustreless his gills and gullet,
His chill gaze like the glazed eyes of a mullet.
'I sometimes feel I have been here before,'
Eunuch vouchsafed.
               'Perhaps during the *War*.
Out *East* when I was rising through the ranks
I would peruse the Classics and give thanks
The Learning which for aeons had descended
To nourish Great Men's minds had not yet ended.
Our Country's cause was just. Who could defeat us?
I came to know myself the son of *Thetis*.
Pale *Tristan*! Great *Beethoven*! They are gone.'
He god by god invoked his pantheon,
While *Britt*'s frenetic biro dashed off dottings
And dotted dashings meant as shorthand jottings.
'The Nation,'
      Eunuch spake,
           'like *Alexander*
Now stands at the *Hydaspes*. Yet we pander
Unblushingly—and here you must excuse
The vehemence, nay violence, of my views—
Indeed I would say spinelessly, to those
(And who they are you know. Everyone knows.)
That would without compunction jeopardize
Our Parliamentary Heritage. Their lies,
And what may well be worse, their endless havering—
Their pusillanimously timid wavering—
Must soon, and I mean *very* soon, endorse—
And this I say with infinite remorse ... '
His wit bombast, his eloquence mere bluster,
A gust of dust the most that he could muster,

(33)

He kept on with his horror-comic oratory —
A footloose *Frankenstein* with no laboratory.
'If I may coin a crude *hapax logomenon*
It is indeed a Frightening Phenomenon
That our most vital Institution cowers
So abjectly while I with all my powers
Of Ratiocination perforce languish,
Unable to assist her in her anguish.
Yet none the less, of course, *et nunc et semper*
A slave to Logic, I shall keep my temper.
Blood in the streets! And through your letter-box —
You must forgive me if my language shocks —
Excreta! Heed the Immigration Figures
Before our land is overrun with ... '
                                        Big as
A house the question loomed: was *Eunuch* cracked?
Alas, nothing so savoury. For in fact
The only plan of campaign through the years
To which this man unswervingly adheres
Is backing any fad that gives him latitude
To strike a solitary Classic attitude.
Behind that flint façade so hieratic
There isn't even a sincere fanatic!
Peripatetic through the reeking flora
Like *Aristotle* in some green Agora
The ageing teacher lectured his apprentice,
Who felt increasingly *non compos mentis*.
Exfoliating round them *Rousseauesquely*
The verdant vegetation coiled grotesquely:
A figment of the mind, a fevered dream,
A swamp where *Enoch Eunuch* reigned supreme.
'Wherever else the action is,'
                            thought *Britt*,
'One thing's for certain. This place isn't it.'

(34)

BOOK FOUR

BRITT's *Eunuch* Profile sparkled with sardonic
Imagination. Its effect was tonic.
Her writing popped and crackled, fizzed and bubbled:
It tickled *Insight* pink but left *Britt* troubled.
Had she been fair? She thought so, since her line
Or argument took care to intertwine
The two opposing views of her new friends:
An artful blend of countervailing trends.
'The Workers,'
        piped *Midge*,
                'basically now dig
That *Eunuch* is a Racist-Fascist pig.'
While *Heidi* trilled:
             'One's absolutely *for* him.
I mean, what else can one *do* but *adore* him?'
Fair, yes. But relevant? *Britt* wasn't sure.
To Politics there must be something more
Than Voices crying in the Wilderness.
Since *Parliament* was just back from Recess,
Perhaps her chance had come to pierce the murk
Of myth and see Democracy at work.
'I doubt you'll find the place exactly thrilling,'
Said *Insight*,
        'But by all means, since you're willing,
Go take a butcher's. Here, you'll need this card.
We'll have lunch when I get back from *Gstaad*.'
Poor *Insight* when he looked at *Britt* looked lost
And often in the lift his skis got crossed:
He'd hang there upside down half crucified
While welders tried to reach him from outside.
All heedless, *Britt* raced off to see the Palace
Of *Westminster* like some up-dated *Alice*
Committed to a course of magic potions

(35)

And pixillated cakes and such-like notions—
Someone resigned to falling down deep holes
And tracing tunnels made by giant moles,
Which lead to countries hitherto unknown—
But stay! The jig is up! The gaff is blown!
For even though the sweet *Thames* softly ran
Below its walls of neo-*Gothic* plan,
And though its windows shimmered in a way
Kokoschka, Turner, Whistler and *Monet*
Combined could not have captured with the brush,
The whole illusion fell flat with a rush
The minute *Britt Bright* got inside and spotted
Those narcoleptic poseurs sparsely dotted
Around the HOUSE OF COMMONS with their feet up—
As proud as small boys peeing with the seat up.
Proponents of Amendments rose and fell.
Opponents of Amendments rose as well,
Proposing the Amendment be amended
Before the Point of Order was suspended.
The burning issue? Value Added Tax,
And how that tax applied to hunting packs.
Should ownership of hounds be Zero-Rated?
For what seemed days the matter was debated
With every clause spelled out letter by letter.
Some Honourable Members thought it better—
And from the hunter's viewpoint much more Viable—
To change the law so that the fox was liable.
The fox would be obliged to keep accounts
Of Inputs, Outputs, dates, times and amounts,
Such records to be quarterly inspected—
And thus the Rights of Dogs would be protected.
(Because here in *Great Britain, God* be thanked,
The Sovereignty of Dogs is sacrosanct:
If pooches were not free to foul the pavement
The Nation would be one step from enslavement,
For if there were no dog-shit on your shoe
You'd know the next to vanish would be you.)
As *Britt* surveyed the dreary scene beneath
She tapped her ball-point pen against her teeth

While inwardly succumbing to a flood
Of *déjà vu* like morphine in the blood.
That cheerless rhetoric! Those hearty antics!
The open warfare waged against semantics!
The helpless *English* tongue gut to the rack!
Les temps retrouvés! How it took her back!
Instead of somewhere just below *Big Ben*
She might have been in *Oxford* once again!
'You see here,'
              said a sharp voice near *Britt*'s ear
So unexpectedly she jumped with fear,
'The death-throes of an Institution. Power
Has now become, to withhold or endower,
The private plaything of the *T.U.C.*
The Unions are our masters. Follow me.'
Britt recognized the freckles and red hair,
The tart tones, foam-flecked lips and pop-eyed stare,
Of JOHN PAUL GINGER, Journalist and Writer—
The right-of-centre Left-wing freedom fighter.
So famed was *John Paul Ginger* both as author
And editor his very name called forth a
Convulsion in *Britannia*'s respiration:
She gasped like the *New Statesman*'s circulation
As down the stairs at *Ginger*'s heels she trotted.
They paused, he shouting, she with stomach knotted,
By *Cromwell*'s statue. *Cromwell* seemed depressed
As if he'd just been privileged to digest
My Lady *Freesia*'s enormous book about him.
(No wonder that he had a mournful look about him,
For *Freesia* had wrapped him up so thick
The paperback was bigger than a brick—
Whence came, no doubt, his aura of
                        'Whoe needes itte?'
Since what use is a Life if no one reads it?
By being too exhaustively revealed
One's fascination simply stays concealed.)
By this time *Ginger* had secured a cab
And off they drove, his glib gift of the gab
Continuously lavished at close range

Upon *Britt*'s shell-like ear.

                                              'Is it not strange
And tragic that his land where *Gloriana*
Once reigned should now be torn like a Banana
Republic by the lawless use of force?
And by a lawless force I mean, of course,
Trade Unions. Wild-cat strikes. The flying picket.
High-jacking. Terrorists. It's just not cricket!'
The cab stopped at the *Hilton*, on whose roof
The Union chiefs that day were giving proof
Of growing influence on World Affairs
By welcoming a *Russian* friend of theirs.
Yes folks! Fresh from the great U.S.S.R.,
The top cat—one might almost say the czar—
Of all Trade Union Members in'a land
Where Working Men take absolute command—
Let's hear it for that Hero of Agrarian
Reform, that huggable Humanitarian,
NIKITA KIKITINSKI! Glasses raised,
The local big-wigs dutifully gazed
In worship at their grim guest where he sat
Still clad in overcoat and black felt hat,
A bulge conspicuous beneath one shoulder.
He stood. He read from a manila folder
While waiters carried in a rather icky
Enormous crimson cake marked 'Hello, Nikki'.
'Your tool-of-*Wall-Street* Capitalist Press
Has struggled night and day without success
To brand me as an enemy of Peace.
They say I'm in the so-called Secret Police!
Bourgeois hyenas! First of all, I'm not.
And second, even if I am, so what?
Such lies! In *Russia*, nobody would dare!
They'd find themselves in ... psychiatric care.'
So saying, *Nikki* glared like a fanatic
And swiftly pulled a silenced automatic.
He took aim at the cake and deftly drilled it
Six times. Instead of cutting it, he killed it!
From half a dozen wounds a hot pink froth

(38)

Of sugar gushed on to the table cloth.
More than a little stunned, it seemed to *Britt*,
The Union heads now rose to do their bit.
LEN MUMBLE, HUGHIE SCREWIE and JACK JOKE
Took turns to talk while *Nikki*, wreathed in smoke,
Subsided with a smile of satisfaction—

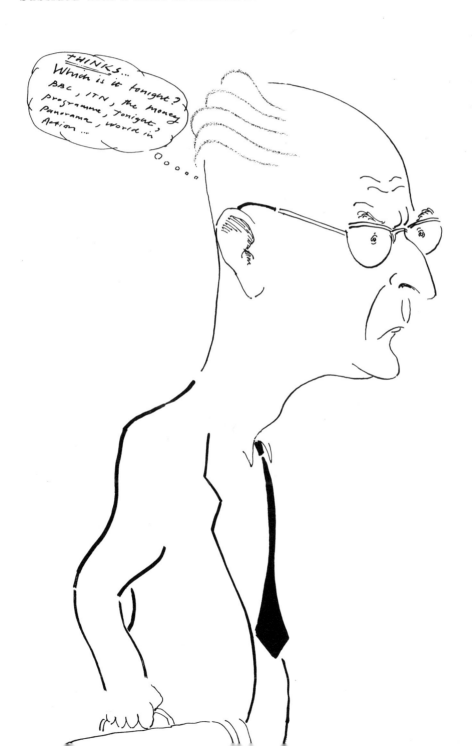

Still *Russia*'s foremost cabaret attraction.
The first to speak was *Mumble*:
                                    'Comrades! Brothers!
Friends, Sisters, Members, Delegates and Others!
In furtherance and legally consecutive
To principles convened by my Executive,
I hereby implement the duly rendered
Decision that the resolutions tendered
To Brother *Kikitinski* with due deference … '
Here *Mumble* stopped. *Joke* started:
                                    'And in reference
To prior previous new indications
Of *ad hoc* overmanning situations
Arising from the Pay Pause differential,
The present Crisis renders it essential
That heretofore pursuant increments … '
Here *Joke* gave way to *Screwie*:
                                    'Must make sense.
This Movement cannot tolerate disparity.
It mitigates against our Solidarity.
Our Militance can only be debilitated
If unanimity is not facilitated.
I therefore, in respect of the said measure,
Reitify with extramural pleasure
Towards this fellow-labourer and martyr
Our thanks *pro tem, pro forma* and *pro rata*.'
Like *Donald Duck*'s three nephews *Hughie, Louie*
And *Dewey*, just so *Mumble, Joke* and *Screwie*
Successively chipped in, each after each,
With separate quotas for the total speech —
A gang of stokers heaving verbal coal,
They fuelled an unrelenting rigmarole.
'You hear that?'
                    Ginger snapped,
                                    'They're in collusion!'
But really all that *Britt* heard was confusion,
Since what they said, though possibly quite sensible,
Was never even briefly comprehensible.
Joe Gormless, Arthur Numscull and *Sid Ghrease*

Were also called upon to say their piece.
Their syntax similarly meretricious,
To *Britt* they still seemed the reverse of vicious.
In fact they'd even started to look harassed—
By *Nikki*'s act perhaps a bit embarrassed.
The pondered the death rattle of the cake
And wondered if they'd made a slight mistake.
Before the wounded icing quite congealed
The speakers found themselves obliged to yield
The floor to yet another honoured guest—
A man conspicuously better-dressed
Than any other Union leader present,
Though in his facial aspect much less pleasant.
CLIVE PERKINS is *Welsh*, waspish, up to date
And always eager to Negotiate.
White-collar workers give thanks for his guile
And on their Union dues he lives in style,
While extra income earned from several sources
Supports a gentlemanly string of horses.
He raucously Backs *Britain* on TV
And drives a *Volvo*, which he gets for free.
'You see,'
          whinged *Perkins* with a knowing smirk,
'The Press don't like the man who does the work.
It's sheer hypocrisy, to say the least,
To call our famous visitor a beast
For being in the *K.G.B.* It's not
As if that lot were different from our lot,
Now is it? Britain's got its *MI6*.
It's all the same, We're up to the same tricks.
You see, the things we say the other side
Are doing, we do too, but try to hide!
Some sentimentalists might make a fuss
But *I* say, what's it got to do with us?
The Media just like a bit of drama.
Now I must leave you, I'm on *Panorama*.'
Britt's biro trembled as she made a note.
A spasm of revulsion gripped her throat
As *Perkins*, to a patter of applause,

Began to move towards the double doors—
Which opened to admit a howling crowd
Of people making their intention loud
And clear that *Nikki* should be quickly sent
Back whence he came. And guess what? *Nikki* went—
Though truly he was sad not to remain.
It pained him to see citizens complain
When he knew so exactly what would suit them.
Too bad that he was not allowed to shoot them.
His helicopter lowered him a rope
And snatched him from the strenuous group grope
Of angry delegates and demonstrators,
Musicians, flunkeys, caterers and waiters.
Yet even as they fought, the air seemed cleaner
And everyone more decent in demeanour,
Including even him who now emerged
From where he'd been propelled when the mob
                                    surged—
Bedecked with cake-crumbs, cream and scarlet icing,
For once *Clive Perkins* looked almost enticing.

BOOK FIVE

BRITT's piece about the dust-up at the *Hilton*
Was of the kind a reputation's built on.
Well-crafted without being overwrought,
In diction flexible, in rhythm taut,
With similes appropriate yet striking
Her prose unrolled to everybody's liking—
Except her own. In fact she felt distressed,
As to her close companion she confessed.
'Dear *Diary*, my thing in today's rag
Came out o.k. I got off the odd gag.
My use of "who" and "whom" was a bit ropy.
They ran a picture of me looking dopy,
But *Harry* subbed my typescript with great care
By phone from *Val d'Isère* and *Sestriere*.
Today I've heard a burst of heavy breathing
From every editor in town. They're seething
With lust to hire the talents of Yours Truly—
I can't say the thought bothers me unduly.
Tomorrow the *New Statesman* buys me lunch
And then on *Wednesday* I'm to lunch at *Punch*.
It looks like I'm as hot as hot can get.
I mean, one's On One's Way. And yet. And yet ... '
While *Midge* and *Heidi* looked at television
Britt sucked her faithful pen with indecision.
'And yet,'
        she went on,
                'I just can't accept
That Politicians can be so inept,
The Workers' representatives so dense.
Somewhere there must be *someone* who talks sense.
I know eventually I'll meet Great Men
And Women. People with Great Minds ... '
                        Just then

(43)

The lolling *Heidi* squealed:

'Ooh, yum yum! Look!'

And *Midge* barked:

'Not *that* Capitalist crook!'

As on the TV screen the face appeared—
Pug-nosed, boss-eyed, flab-jowled, big-mouthed,
   jug-eared—
Of QUINTIN SWINE, LORD HOGWASH. He was grinning
And pouting in a manner he thought winning,
While with a reverent air *Joan Brakeball* whined:
'*Lord Hogwash*, you've been called the Finest Mind
In Politics Today. A thinking *Tory*
Who none the less bows down before *Christ*'s glory.
Please tell us something now about your view
Of *God*. I mean, what does He mean to you?'
'Good Heavens,'

snorted *Hogwash*,

'everything.

Who else *is* there? To what else can one cling?
For never mind how slippery the slope,
God, Queen and *Country* always give us hope.
The artists, too. *Van Braque. Fantin-Lautrec.*
Gaugogh. Gaugas? Forget which. Have to check.
A sense of lasting values. Nothing squalid.
That feeling of the spiritually solid
Without whose help we'd face the cataclysm—
The rising tide of anarchy and schism—
Unarmed. This thing in *Cyprus*. The Cod War.
Plaid Cymru. The declining rule of law.
These go-slows organized by *Moscow*'s minions.
Sit-ins. Brain drains. Pop groups. The *Palestinians*.
These muggings on the Tube. The *Lebanon*.
And all this Streaking that's been going on.
Let no one say I am equating these.
Such facts you must interpret as you please.
I simply make appeal to common reason
And sum up in one word. That word is: TREASON!
The whole damned shooting match has gone to *Hell*!
And now I think it's time I rang my bell.'

(44)

He made a brazen noise while *Brakeball* smiled
And nodded as if humouring a child.
Britannia, though, had long since swooned away,
To wake late in the morning of next day.
She dressed in haste and raced in consternation
Down *Ken. High Street* in search of transportation.
A cab that looked already occupied
Hove to beside her.

         'Miss *Bright*! Want a ride?'
A voice called from within. She took a peek
And climbed inside, too overwhelmed to speak.
Her Good *Samaritan* was JERRY MERRY,

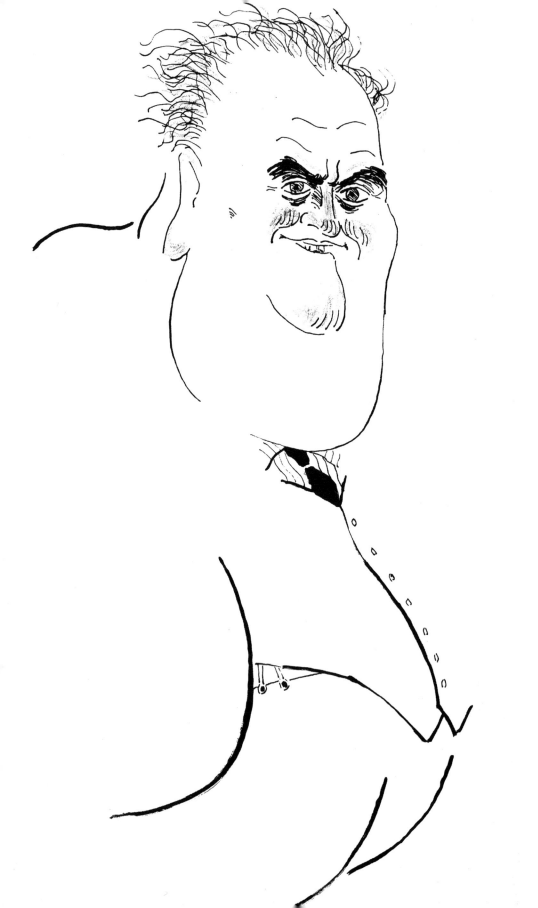

The *Liberal* Party Leader. He looked very
Impressive in his waistcoat, watch and chain,
Grey homburg, spats and silver-headed cane.
His blasé air, loose-limbed and heavy-lidded,
Was doubly to be praised when you considered
Whom he was crammed into the back seat with—
All his M.P.s, including 'SIRLOIN' SMITH,
A figure of *avoirdupois* so awesome
That on his own he counted as a foursome.
What games! The *Liberal* Parliamentary Presence
Packed tighter than a basket full of pheasants!
And CLEMENT DOGFOOD said:
                              'Glad you could come,
Britannia. Would you like a plate of *"Chum"*?'

And there *John Prodlow* sat, and *David Sleet*,
And then ... But soon the roster was complete,
For really, despite all the grunt and jostle,
As Parties go theirs wasn't too colossal:
The number, when you sorted out the jumble,
Of personnel involved was pretty humble.
You'd not have thought it, though, to hear their Chief.
His black-rimmed eyes were brilliant with Belief.
To hear him talk, the Member for *North Devon*
Was well along the way to Seventh *Heaven*.
'Our sights are set beyond mere Coalition,'
Said *Merry*.
                    'I was offered high position,
But soon saw through their ruse. To capture me—
Who in my youth sat on *Lloyd George*'s knee—
Would take more Parliamentary *savoir faire*
Than anyone nowadays has got to spare.
Oh *Asquith*! *Simon*! *Samuel*! They were giants.
Where are they now?'
                              His dark eyes flashed defiance.
You would have thought, to judge from his deep look,
Tradition was to him an open book—
Though really he'd not been the best of students
And only took a *Third* in *Jurisprudence*.
'We shall go on towards a *Liberal Britain*,'
Said *Merry*.
                    '*Britain* now's weak as a kitten,
Its Parliamentary system quite outmoded.'
Britt found his Credibility corroded:
Tall talk about Tomorrow was in vain—
His love of Yesterday was all too plain.
They turned into *High Holborn*. *Britt* protested:
'You're miles out of your way,'
                                        but she was bested.
'Let's not',
                    said *Merry*, tapping the partition,
'Be bound by a too rigid sense of mission.
We don't know where we're going. We just go.'
'Young *Jerry*'s a comedian, as you know,'

(48)

Laughed *'Sirloin' Smith*.

        'Still, we'll take care of him.'
And for a moment *Merry*'s glance grew dim,
But *Britt* was in *Great Turnstile* running fast,
And didn't see the sudden shadow cast
In those fine features as his time grew shorter —
A dark sigh like a squall across the water.
The *Statesman*'s Editor was HOWARD HORRID,
A homely youth behind whose bulbous forehead
There ticked a brain of formidable quickness.
'How do *you* diagnose Our Current Sickness?'
He asked *Britannia* in an urgent voice
While offering a somewhat narrow choice
Of sandwiches.

       'But first, would you like ham —
At least I think it's ham. It could be spam —
Or curried egg? We have to watch expenses.
Extravagance has drastic consequences.'
The office door burst open to admit
A man whom *Horrid* introduced to *Britt*
With something less than pride.

          '*Britannia Bright*,
JOHN GALLSTONE. How's it going, *John*? All right?'
The tycoon held a typescript with both hands.
It fluttered as he read.

        'Justice demands
That I speak out on how I have been treated,
And how this country tortures the defeated.
What was I guilty of? Originality.
Defiance of conventional morality.
And now I'm victimized not just with jail
But something even more vindictive. Bail.
I'm arbitrarily denied release
According to some strange whim of the police.
Oh *England*! How you persecute the bold,
The dauntless buccaneers who bring you gold!
I fear my future now lies in *Australia*,
Which hails me as a rebel, not a failure.
They know out there how *Britain* has conspired

To crush the finest sons it ever sired.
Farewell, my doomed land!'

                      Britt was almost gripped
As *Gallstone* plonked his tatty manuscript
On *Horrid*'s desk and hummed *Waltzing Matilda*.
He turned and left.

                'A circulation builder,'
Said *Horrid*,

           'I'm afraid we need his name.'

And *Britt* saw *Horrid* hang his head for shame,
Though in a moment up it bobbed once more.
'But to return to what I said before:
You're young, progressive, pretty, full of verve—
Is *Britain* run the way that you deserve?'
And *Britt* replied:
                         'I've simply not a clue.
Is someone running it? *Please* tell me who.'
Here consternation entered *Horrid*'s face.
'Of course they are. You've looked in the wrong place.
The Party Conferences decide what matters.
That's where the boot goes in and the blood spatters.
The crunch of bones. The hair torn out in tufts.
Tomorrow it's the *Tories*. They're at *Crufts*.
I think you'd capture the occasion's flavour
In just the way our readership would savour.'
Before *Britt* could reply, they heard a thump
From far off, but enough to make them jump.
Britt found herself a bit less than elated.
For quite a while they both stood still and waited.
Then *Horrid* brought the meeting to a close
And sat down to rewrite *John Gallstone*'s prose.

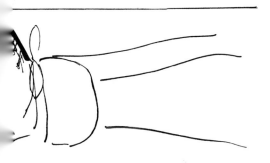

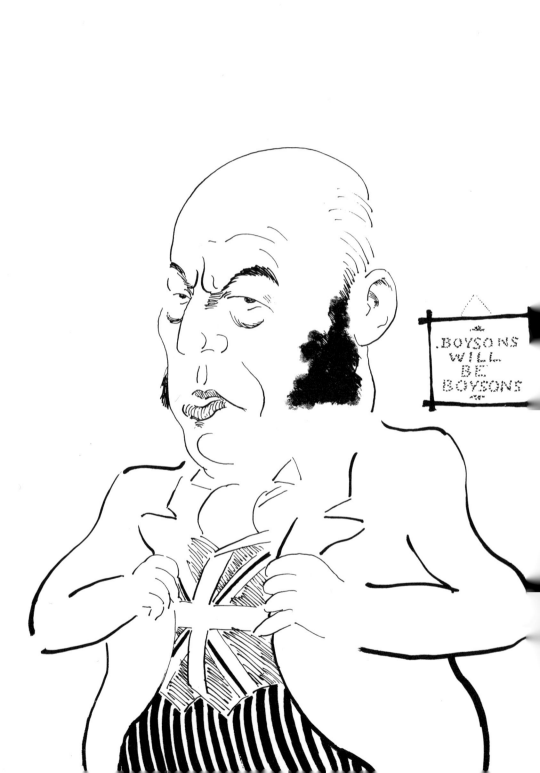

BOOK SIX

CRUFTS and *Conservatism* go together
Like corgis collared to a common tether.
Olympia's the site of the event
And thither the next day *Britannia* went,
Mad keen to see high-minded Politicians
Defending their Political Positions,
Not for their own, but for the People's sake,
In friendly Democratic give and take.
The floor of the great hall was fairly teeming—
Flags waving, whistles blowing, streamers streaming—
As myriads of *Tories* mingled cheerfully
(For being with their own kind pleased them fearfully)
And marked their cards and fought to place their bets
On candidates adorned with large rosettes.
The grand prize was the Party Leadership—
A post on which TED TEDE still kept his grip,
But only just. Was this his fatal year?
His shoulders shook with mirth. Or was it fear?
The race was on. While *Britt* sat tight and watched
Preliminary judging quickly scotched
The chances of the has-beens and back-benchers.
Lynx-eyed adjudicators measured dentures
And pinched fat cheeks and ruthlessly discriminated
Till all but the most perfect were eliminated.
Too dry of tongue or too wet in the muzzle,
The also-rans fell out. A hopeless puzzle
To *Britt*, who found the sporting terminology
As abstruse as Molecular Biology,
So while the lesser lights went through their paces
She killed time putting names to famous faces.
She saw *Old Mac McHack*, still looking well;
She saw and heard *Lord Hogwash*, with his bell;
And that thing, she could not help but assume,

Had once been called *Sir Ancient Stately-Home*.
Two ex-*Prime Ministers* and one near miss—
The Elder Statesmen rubbing elbows! Bliss.
And back there, looking grave or was it bored,
Was *Airy Wave* or was it *Agnes Maude*.
Why was it that Right Wingers looked disdainful?
Was breathing other people's air so painful?
And standing on a soap-box like a preacher
Was *Enoch Eunuch*, spouting pearls from *Nietzsche*.
Rough furs he wore, and skins and thongs and things:
The helmet on his head had little wings.
And *Michael Muscletone*, so full of thrust,
Looked hard to stop if harder still to trust;
And there *Rholls Royson*, seething with dissension,
Had made himself the centre of attention;

And there was *Reggie Mudling*, half awake,
Extolling *Malta* to *Lord Ecclescake*;
And *St John Stiltheels*, loose-limbed with euphoria,
Dressed in the underwear of *Queen Victoria*.
All these and more *Britt* recognized and noted
While rattles rattled, toilet paper floated,
Balloons went up, confetti fell like rain,
And flashbulbs popped like bubbles in champagne.
By now, their toothy smiles assessed for brilliance,
Their thighs for plumpness, buttocks for resilience,
The field-within-a-field had been selected.
The contents of their sand-trays were inspected
And from their ranks were culled the tiny few
Prospective champions who would go through
To face the final stretch of the formalities—

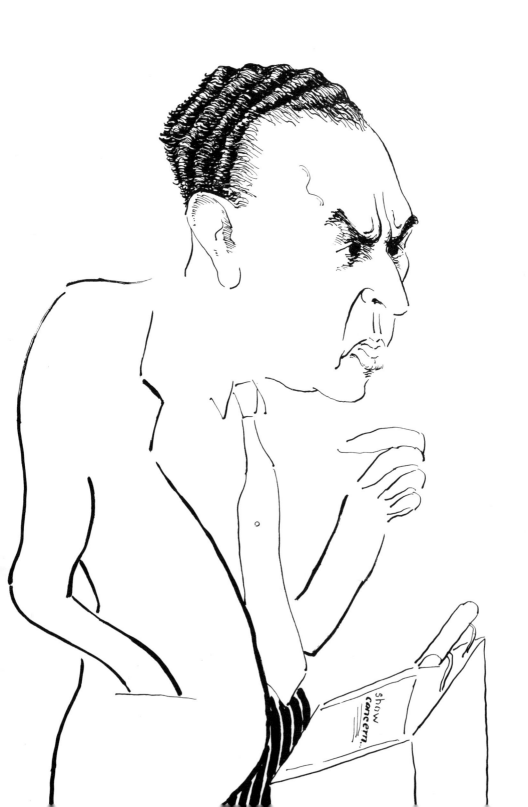

A set speech to reveal their Personalities.
A sudden hush. A press-roll on the snare.
A crisp heraldic fanfare split the air.
A blazing cone of light picked up the dais
Like that white radiance in *Adonais*,
And there, with kinky hair and bulging eyes,
KEITH YOYO stood, impenetrably wise.
His voice was deep, his thoughts were even deeper:
He wasn't allowed out without a keeper.
'This *Labour* Government has plainly lost,'
Said *Yoyo*,
      'any grasp of the true cost
To *Britain* of their fiscal prodigality.
Their policies are crimes against morality—
Sheer waste which can no longer be afforded.'
The audience was with him. It applauded.
'A workable distinction must be found
Between the Middle and the Common Ground.

(57)

The Common Ground is different from the Middle:
That much is clear.'
                          But it was still a riddle.
'Wealth-Eating Public Sector overspending,'
He went on,
                  'stands revealed as outward-tending.
The feedback of the spiral is now leading
The put-down up to meet itself receding.'
The audience was stumped. Though it still clapped,
The strength of its response was somewhat sapped.
'I strongly recommend a plus-flow vector
To aid the Wealth-Creating Private Sector
And thereby keep abreast of what we need.
We'll pay the Lower Orders not to breed!'
This last thought was a big hit, but by now
It seemed high time that *Yoyo* took a bow.
The more his rhodomontade waxed rabbinical
The more his aspect bordered on the clinical.
A large vein in his temple started throbbing.
He faltered in mid-flight. He started sobbing.
He beat his forehead with his fist and railed
Against himself:
                  'I failed! I failed! I failed!'
He went off on a stretcher. The sensation
Aroused by every finalist's oration
Was registered on one of BOB MCKEEN's
Amazing Psephological Machines.
In *Yoyo*'s case the arrow pscarcely pstirred,
Which more or less meant he had got the bird.
'No swing for *Yoyo*,'
                      said *McKeen* intensely.
'Stay tuned, however. Things could change immensely.'
Next up was WILLY WHITEFISH, a Stout Fellow
Whose mealy mouth gave forth a mellow bellow.
Moon-faced like some slow creature of the deep,
Although wide-eyed, he still seemed half asleep:
Yet when you poked him underneath the blubber
You found out he was made of ... well, of rubber.
'You all know me: an average sort of chappie,'

(58)

Said *Whitefish*, sadly trying to look happy.
'Fair-mindedness is really all I care for
And frankly I believe that's what I'm there for.
Not, certainly, ambition. Dear me, no.
Oh dear me, not at all. Yo ho ho ho.'
Here *Whitefish* jiggled his array of jaws
And did his best to look like *Santa Claus*.
'I have my critics, yes. I bear no grudge.
But from my principles I shall not budge.
I'm just a normal type, as I've been saying,
But none the less this is no game we're playing.
I shan't give way. Oh very well, I shall.
So vote for Moderation. Be a pal.'
Prolonged applause and shouts of
                                        'Well rowed, *Willie*!'
But *Bob*'s Machine went only slightly silly.
His Pointer strained and trembled but fell back
Till finally it hung there looking slack
As ROBIN BRAY chimed in:
                                        'And at this stage
It's *Whitefish* over *Yoyo*, but *Bob*'s Gauge
Still shows uncertainty. Is that right, *Bob*?'

'Right, *Robin*,'
        said *Bob*,
                'but from now the job
Gets easier. It's for the kind of hand
TED TEDE receives that my Machine was planned.
See what I mean?'
            His eager Needle twitched
And flickered round and round as if bewitched:
For now, to sounds of thousands going wild,
TED TEDE appeared. He smiled. He waved. He smiled.
He waved and smiled. He waved and smiled again.
He waved and smiled and waved and smiled and then
He shook as if he'd just been told a joke
And waved and smiled and waved and smiled and
                        spoke.
'You all,'
      said *Tede*,
              'know what Last Time was like.
We had the Three Day Week, the Miners' Strike ...
This Time I guarantee there'll be good news.
This Time will be a different pair of shoes.
I promise you a whole new Me. Less Shyness,
With Warmth and Fun in place of the old Dryness.
The old ice-cold demeanour will be axed.
Instead, I shall be utterly Relaxed.'
He waved and smiled. The groundlings went berserk.
New-Formula *Ted Tede* was now at work!
'But underneath,'
        quoth *Tede*,
                'I'll still be steel.
Beneath the velvet glove, the iron heel.
No matter how I'm slandered and betrayed
By those around me, I am unafraid.
I still retain my optimistic mood—
With one or two close friends to taste my food.'
The thought was getting harder to avoid
That *Tede* might be a wee bit paranoid.
'Vote for the man,'
        boomed *Tede*,

During the *Suez* Crisis—on the Whip.
You didn't catch *me* running round resigning.
It's not my style to waste my time repining.
The *E.E.C.*, for instance. I did that.
I'll be *P.M.* again or eat my hat.
Pick me, and at a stroke we shall have won—
So just make bloody sure you get that done.'
Bob's Indicator took off like a rocket:
It spun so fast it rattled in its socket.
'It's looking good for *Tede*,'

                  cried *Bob* ecstatically,
But *Robin* viewed the data less dramatically
And sagely cautioned:

              'Bob, let's not forget
Ted Tede now meets his biggest challenge yet.
Can MARGO HATBOX jolt him from top spot?
Or is there something *Margo* hasn't got?'
The audience made noises like *Niagara*.
A woman finely drawn as some *Tanagra*
Or *Dresden* figurine was now preparing
To give her kit of axioms an airing.
Her skin peaches and cream, her hair spun gold,
Cucumber-cool with eyeballs ice-cube cold,
She looked like the epitome of poise—
A schoolgirl twice as grown-up as the boys.
Composed of swoops and condescending trillings,
A voice like silver paper on your fillings
Emerged abruptly from the massed loudspeakers.
'We all of us,'

      Hatbox began,

                 'are Seekers
Of Freedom. I am too. Oh gracious yes.
And yet we'll never cure our present mess
Unless we stop this notion we've been giving
The idle that the world owes them a living.
The Welfare system needs to be re-modelled.
Malingerers are being molly-coddled!'
The huge crowd was already on its feet

And stamping so hard *Britt* bounced in her seat.
'Good gracious me,'
                         cried *Hatbox* through the din,
'The time has come to bring back Discipline.
For *Heaven*'s sake let's end this Aimless Drift
And start rewarding those who practise Thrift.
We need to back the Workers, not the Shirkers.
And if that fails we should send in the *Gurkhas*.'
The congregation, whinnying like mares,
Were making bonfires out of stacks of chairs.
Bob's Pointer whirred and blurred and disappeared
And flew in fragments as its bearing sheared.
'Well, *Robin*,'
                  yelled *Bob*,
                                'nothing could be clearer.'
'Yes, *Bob*,'
                 yelled *Robin*,
                                  'it's a whole new era.'
By sycophants and catamites surrounded
The victrix seemed well pleased but not astounded:
The hearty handshakes and festoons of flowers
She took as fitting tribute to her powers.
Ted Tede looked woebegone. His loss had stunned him.
He waved and smiled and waved but *Hatbox* shunned
                                                    him.

The revelry took ages to subside
While poor *Tede* almost died of injured pride.
His farewell speech was mainly about boats
And better days when he got all the votes.
With bravely weathered helm and cracking sail
He scudded with his stern turned to the gale.
With creaking yards set square across the mast
He ran before the vast blast from the past.
With prow and poop staved in by giant seas
He foundered in typhoons of memories —
And then the sky grew clear on peaceful scenes
Of seagulls feeding on the might-have-beens.

BOOK SEVEN

'How super! Though of course one's sad for *Ted*,'
Said *Heidi* as the troika went to bed.
'It's great,'
       groaned *Midge*,
                    'to see a Woman make it,
But as a Radical I just can't take it.'
They snuggled deep beneath the *Slumberdown*.
'Dear *Diary*,'
       Britt scribbled with a frown,
'I hope that next week's *Labour* Conference brings
Me nearer to the vital heart of things.
The *Tory* gig was just a family feud.
I almost felt embarrassed to intrude,
With old *Ted* going down without a ripple
And *Margo* in that hat like a whale's nipple.
Good copy, though. My piece was fun to write,
And darling *Howard* went mad with delight.'
He did indeed. So did they all. *Britt*'s byline
Was now a fixture in the *Fleet Street* skyline.
The name *Britt Bright* was something you could see on
A dozen buildings written up in neon.
The Editors were wining her and dining her
And suavely pulling contracts out and signing her
Until she was so thoroughly snowed under
She felt that she was being pulled asunder.
The lunch at *Punch* was really just the start.
There WILHELM KAISER tried to win her heart
By telling jokes which left her at a loss,
Such as:
       'Vy did der chicken der road cross?'
LORD BOOBY was there too, to beat his breast
About his visit to the *Eagle's Nest*.
'At this point *Hitler* screamed as if in pain,

(67)

And I thought: *Booby,* this man is insane.'
Lord Booby capped his story with a burp.
Beside him sat the bow-tied *Wyatt Twerp,*
A *Labour* rebel who had turned up late
Because he always brought his own gold plate.
It's heavy stuff to get down from the shelf—
The same shelf *Twerp* had been left on himself.
ST MALCOLM MOTHERMILK was there to boot,
Replete with parables he thought astute
About the shameful pointlessness of satisfying
The senses he had spent a lifetime gratifying.
'Our task must be to copy *Kierkegaard,'*
Said *Mothermilk,*

                'and I've tried very hard.
The effort only can increase one's utter

Obeisance to *Teresa* of *Calcutta*.
And yet this lust for things machines can measure,
This electronic calculus of pleasure,
This mix-up of *mons pubis* and *mens sana*,
This *Masters-Johnson* nightmare of *Nirvana*—
Beside what's going on in *Bangla Desh*,
How meaningless these frenzies of the flesh
Now seem. This claret … is there any more?'
And BRIEN BORON said:
                  'I'm *not* a bore,
Am I? I'm *not* a bore. At *Private Eye*
They're saying I'm a bore. I wonder why?'
That wasn't all he said, or rather sang:
I give you just the tang of his harangue.
The sighing table was addressed by *Boron*—

A well-read man whom whisky made a moron —
Till people found it more than they could bear
And fell asleep into the sole *meunière*.
The gossip *Nigel Dampstain* stayed awake,
Informing *Britt* that he proposed to take
Her off to *Private Eye* to catch the last
Of what that paper deemed a fit repast.
He didn't look too trustworthy, but still …
She acquiesced. They set off up the hill,
With *Dampstain* slyly pumping her for torrid
Intelligence concerning her and *Horrid*.
Did *Insight* still stand high in her affection?
His probing was like verbal vivisection.
Britt noticed *Dampstain*'s shoes squelched as he talked.
Small puddles formed behind him as he walked,
And on his hand, she now saw with a shiver,
Those little spots she'd thought were caused by liver
Were moving. They must be some kind of lice.
No, *Nigel Dampstain* wasn't very nice.
In *Greek Street* they went upstairs in a pub
That serves the *Private Eye* team as a club.
They found a trestle table thinly laid
With gruel and viands of a lowly grade.
But *Britt* was overawed, for it was here
The *Eye* crew had their fortnightly Idea,
And here now *Richard Inkwell* sat in splendour —
His manner strangely diffident and tender,
Considering his literary stance.
Like all his colleagues, *Inkwell* wore short pants,
Long stockings and a cap with the School crest —
An Old *Salopian* must look his best.
Beside him crouched that hard case and tough nut,
The far-Left free-lance journalist PAUL PHUTT,
Who told *Britt Oxford* was
                                'a Tragic Farce,
A privileged *enclave* of the Ruling Class.'
But *Britt* thought this was going a bit far.
Had *Phutt* himself not been an *Oxford* star?
And pray what Class was his if not the Ruling?

She wondered who this man thought he was fooling.
And further down the table sat *Bron Wan*,
Who saw *Britt* and was straightaway far gone:
His clownish noggin swivelled on its pivot
So rapidly it almost popped a rivet.
He gave up working on his latest column
And sat there looking fathomlessly solemn,
Since underneath his pose as a harsh realist
Bron Wan was an incurable idealist
Who saw reality as mere futility,
And hence told lies about it with facility.
But now *Bron* on his own petard was hoist:
Installed below the salt, *Dampstain* rejoiced,
His pencil busy with this new romance.
And suddenly *Britt*'s agitated glance
Absorbed the fact that what she'd thought was grime
On *Dampstain*'s neck was more akin to slime,
Deposited by beetles, blue-black bugs
And grey, pulsating, purple-spotted slugs,
Which now and then emerged to leave their dirt
And then went back to breed beneath his shirt.

And over this ménage *Inkwell* presided
As if it should be praised and not derided.
The dull, the dodgy, the downright despicable —
His tolerance of these was inexplicable,
Or marked a man who'd mocked the world so long
He'd ceased to care if he was right or wrong.
The afternoon dragged on into the night.
Britt dashed from Left to Right to Ultra-Right.
The *Bertorelli Blackshirts* lionized her.
The hit-men at *Encounter* idolized her.
A chorus of *Black Paper* literati
Announced that they were starting their own Party,
And into this *John Brainwave, Bernard Beaver*
And *Kingsley Kong* were eager to receive her.
For six days on the trot *Britannia* lunched
Until her rump was sore, her spine was hunched.
For six nights running she went out and ate
And hobnobbed with the great and got home late.

(73)

'How fabulous,'

   sighed *Heidi* as they supped.

'The System's got you,'

    Midge hissed.

       'You're corrupt.'

Vere Hamstrung, Rupert Mudrake and MAX AXE—

Press Barons such as these *Britt* met in stacks.

'I hate the *Hun*,'

   said *Max Axe*, looking rugged.

'I go for him.'

   And *Britt* thought:

       'I'll be buggered.'

She met the famous editor *Dens-Fogg*,

Who showed what can be done by sheer hard slog.

Dens-Fogg wrote canting letters to his son
The way he thought *Lord Chesterfield* had done.
He served them up again as editorials
That weighed down on your soul like war memorials.
(*God* help the humourless! Of all their crimes
Amongst the worst is editing *The Times*.)
The *Beau Monde* welcomed *Britt* with open arms
Whose hands had painted nails and pampered palms.
Britt heard them as *Odysseus* heard the Siren—
Those fashionable people whom *Lord Byron*
Somewhere describes (and, in describing, dooms)
As Fifteen Hundred Fillers of Hot Rooms.

It was at *Highrise House* one night she met
LORD CHIFFCHAFF.
                    'To contain the Russian Threat,'
Said *Chiffchaff* with a statesmanlike clairvoyance,
'We must, I fear, submit to the annoyance
Of placing Freedom under some restriction,
In order to reduce internal friction.
We should take steps. I don't say what they are.
I merely point to my good friend the *Shah*.'
Thus clever lads who make it to the top
Start saying social discontent should stop.
By *Lady Highrise Britt* was introduced
To cocky men who liked to rule the roost.
LORD PITPROP talked of how he'd run the mines:
Sir Richard Swamp about his railway lines.
Lord Pitprop said:
            'I should have been *P.M.*'

Swamp said the same. And that's enough of *them,*
Since neither of them scored much more than gamma
Compared to the unarguable glamour
Of such well-groomed and yet go-getting men
As *Nigel Nylon,* chief of *I.T.N.*—
Whose taste for high-born ladies didn't hamper
A knack for finding dogsbodies to scamper
Around the world with *Arriflexes* whirring.
They caught whatever news might be occurring
While back in *London Nylon* held the fort,
To titled women paying tireless court.
One brilliant evening *chez Wee Georgie Wide*
Britt Bright found *Nigel Nylon* at her side.
A certain possibility was mooted.
She thought, said Yes, and found herself recruited.
At dawn next day her new career began.
At *Heathrow,* freshly flown from *Pakistan,*
TARIQ EL FRIQ faced *Britt Bright*'s microphone.
Apart from her news crew, they were alone:
El Friq's old friends had not turned up to greet him.
The Revolution hadn't come to meet him!
'By George! I see the System has repressed
Our Movement,'

        cried *El Friq.*

                  'I shall not rest
Until I am effecting the release
Of all my comrades now held by the police
In concentration camps throughout the Nation.'
El Friq had not yet grasped that with Inflation
The Counter-Culture had become past tense:
Such fancies wax and wane with Affluence.
Britt talked to the *Scots Communist,* JIM CREED
A formidable-looking man indeed,
Who showed her through some frightful block of flats
With fine words like:

                'The rat-race is for rats.'
How awkwardly his gentle heart assorted
With all those crimes he tacitly supported!
And yet *Jim Creed* might take his rightful place

(79)

The day Compassion rules the human race—
Though for that day to come we're waiting still,
And in my time I think it never will.
With all these luminaries *Dampstain* frantically
Attempted to link *Britt*'s fair name romantically,
But let the real facts here be underlined:
Her one true love was MAGNUS MASTERMIND,
Who'd left the *B.B.C.* and gone to war
To captain the *Icelandic* gun-boat *Thor*,
Which fought the *British* Navy on its tod
So *Reykjavik* might hold on to its cod.
On *Thor*'s cold deck *Britt Bright* was dropped by
                                        chopper,

Slipped on the ice and almost came a cropper,
But soon felt safe—she never had felt better—
Thrust up against the oily roll-neck sweater
Of *Captain Mastermind*, whose flaxen hair
Streamed like a *Viking*'s in the freezing air.
'Your special subject, it appears, is me,'
Said *Mastermind*. Outside in the green sea
The pack-ice stretched away on either bow.
'First question: what is this I'm doing now?'
Upon a pile of life-belts *Britt* lay back
And whispered:
              'Pass.'
              Then everything went black.

BOOK EIGHT

'**D**EAR *Diary*, it's been a marvellous week,'
Wrote *Britt*.
     '*Lord Chiffchaff* and *Tariq El Friq*:
How different! And yet somehow, how the same!
Each in his way a Keeper of the Flame!
And as for *Magnus* ... well, I bear the traces.'
She kept on finding fish-scales in strange places.
'I've been to the Political Extremes.
I've run the gamut. So, at least, it seems:
And yet I've still not seen who calls the tune.
God willing that will all change very soon:
The *Labour* Conference starts tomorrow night.'
And where, you'll all be asking, was the site—
Earl's Court or *Balls's Halls* or *Wembley Stadium?*
No, none of those. Where else but the PALLADIUM?
'Good evening, welcome!'
     shouted DAVID DROSS,
'To start the Show, comedian *Clay Cross*
Will warm you up as only he can do—
And then, rock music from the *Shrewsbury Two*!
So let's lie back and laugh and eat our sweets
While all you late arrivals find your seats.'
The stalwart *Labour* Party rank and file
Packed out the stalls and crowded every aisle,
An audience of names *Britt* didn't know:
The famous names were mostly in the Show.
But wait a moment. Wasn't that man there—
The haughty one who plainly didn't care
Whose toes he trod on as he pushed along
And seemed to relish being in the wrong—
The Thinker TONY CROSSLINE? His cheroot
Kept calm while bones were crushed beneath his boot.
In *Crossline*'s case, behaving very badly

(81)

Is always called Not Suffering Fools Gladly;
His blend of arrogance and indecision
Is lauded as Complexity of Vision;
And even though he'd once been known to say
In cold print:

        'We must all learn to be gay,'
The years had made it clear that the gay life
Means life in *Holland Park* with a smart wife,
The Public Sector staved off with a dollop—
And, if your bluff is called, you cry:

                'Codswallop!'
And there sat *Eric Effing*, Super-Prole,
His clumsy mouth an ever-open hole
From which ill-tempered platitudes were blurted
And into which his foot was oft inserted.

Beside him sat the Chief Whip, *Robert Mulish*,
Who from his way of talking might seem foolish,
Small-minded, cold-souled, bullying and boring,
And in fact is. Beside him there sat snoring
That big man at *Securicor, Ray Grunter*;
And then, accepting money from a punter,
The bookie *Mick the Kard*, who had two heads—
One which condemned Aggression by the *Reds*,
The other which, with less noise and more tact,
Did deals in timber with the *Warsaw Pact*.
So *Mick the Kard* had shirts made with two necks
And always carried a spare pair of specs.
Lord Cowcud ambled in and sat alone—
For next to him was *Willy Hecklethrone*,
Engulfed in a great heap of documents

(84)

Which proved the *Monarchy* had no defence
Against the charge that it cost lots of cash—
A fact with which he hoped to make a splash.
And there *Sir Manny Chinwag* sat enamoured
Of all the sounds his voice made when he yammered,
While *Shirley Whirley* hurried in with miles
And miles of memos, ledgers, notes and files.
The zany way she tripped and fell was charming.
The spread of information was alarming.
Roy Rattlesnake did not leap to assist—
Perhaps because he was a Pragmatist.
But now the orchestra played massive chords:
Britt saw the Union Leaders take the boards.
Joke, Screwie, Numscull, Gormless, Ghrease and *Mumble*
In sequinned taffeta, without a stumble,

Laid on a demonstration of Formation
Facilitated Wage Negotiation!
Split-shift anomalies were circumvented!
Decisive steps were fully implemented!
The stage was a cascade of whirling gowns
And unintelligible abstract nouns!
'Fantastic, super, just great. Weren't they great?'
Sang *Dross*,

        'And now I know you just can't wait
To meet that great man whom we all hold dear,
ROY JUNKET! Great. *Roy*, great to have you here.'
Long, long ago the son of a *Welsh* miner,
Roy Junket now aspires to something finer:
The drawing-rooms he visits are luxurious.
Which doesn't mean his principles are spurious,
Just that they've undergone an Evolution—
A common one, unlike his elocution.
'I wise tonight not welishing my wole,'
Said Junket with much agony of soul.
'The weason I have once again wesigned
Is, I weitewate, the daily gwind.
The *Wefewendum* was a sepawate wealm:
One weckoned weckless hands had gwasped the helm.
But now I must—I'm sowwy to sound dweawy—
Wegwetfully weveal I have gwown weawy,
Since even for the stwong fwame of a stwipling
To be *Home Secwetawy* would be cwippling.
When one has overstwained one's concentwation
One's only wecourse is wecupewation.
I hope to find welief for my wacked muscles
As *Bwitain*'s wepwesentative in *Bwussels*.'
Applause showed that they all already missed him:
All but *Babs Bustle*, who jumped up and hissed him.
She thought that *Roy* had cut short her career.
(He had, too, but that's neither there nor here.)
'Fantastic, super, marvellous, thank you, *Roy*,'
Wailed *Dross*,

        'And now you'll all go mad with joy
I know, to meet a man you love to like—

(86)

It's MICHAEL PHUTT. Great, Super. Take, it, *Mike*.'
Below a mane of hair, behind large glasses,
That Champion of the Exploited Classes
Swept forward with his pinched lips gleaming whitely,
Nye Bevan's Mantle wrapped around him tightly
As if he'd just been blown in by a gale
Of workers' grievances from *Ebbw Vale*,
His rage on their behalf no whit abated
By finding out he was the one they hated.
'You all well know it is with deep remorse,'
Said *Phutt* in tears,
                            'that I must take this course.
Employment Ministers find no enjoyment
In generating further Unemployment,
Especially when, let alone create it,
They've always said they'd never tolerate it.
I thought of quitting. Often. Yet at length
I searched within myself and found the strength
To stay on and support this Government.
But rest assured: I very nearly went.'
He bowed. The mighty audience was hushed,
By retroactive apprehension crushed.
Phutt turned away towards the off-Prompt wing.
He moved one foot but could not seem to bring
The other up to join it. He remained.
The audience's Love was unrestrained:
Applause went on and on and on and on
And at the end of it he'd *still* not gone.
'Just great. And now let's take another look,'
Raved *Dross* as *Phutt* was hauled off with a hook,
'At someone half *Marconi*, half *Karl Marx* —
Yes, TONY WEDGTAIL TITT. *Now* we'll see sparks.'
Equipped with sandwich and pint mug of tea,
The man in question was a sight to see.
No one could be, it seemed to the awed *Britt*,
More Down to Earth than *Tony Wedgtail Titt*.
That *Titt* must be a thoughtful sort of type
You gathered from the way he sucked his pipe.
You knew it wasn't Trendy-Left baloney

When this man gruffly said:
                        'Just call me *Tony.'*
He'd chucked his place among the Landed Gentry.
He'd ruthlessly pruned back his *Who's Who* entry.
He threw his front door open when you rang
And warmly said:
                        'Hi. Come and join the gang.'
No, call him dilettante, call him devil,
This diehard Leveller was on the level.
'With every passing day this Country's health,'
Said *Titt,*
                'demands we fairly share our Wealth,
And it has been in Wealth's redistribution
This Government has worked a Revolution.
It's clear that if the Public stands the loss
The Public has the right to be the boss.
To help a sinking ship regain its grip
We charge a stiff price: Public Ownership.
Whichever large concerns get in a mess
The Public must eventually possess.
As one by one the industries go bust
The People will fork out their hard-earned crust,
And simply by assuming all the debts
Create a mighty empire of bad bets,
Until, when the whole thing's gone to the wall,
We ordinary folk will own it all!
Yes, when it's all collapsed we'll run the lot!
And all it takes is everything we've got!'
Titt laughed a crazy laugh and turned lime-green.
There was a puff of smoke where he had been.
Fantastic. What an artist. What a trouper,'
Yelled *Dross.*
                'That's *Tony Titt.* Amazing. Super.
And now we've got the most surprising act
In showbiz since *Pearl Harbour* was attacked,
That Mad Mixed Marriage of Mild Mirth and Menace,
Who else but JOKIN' JIM and DISMAL DENIS?'
The two came on in lock-step waving boaters
And did the dance with which they wowed the voters.

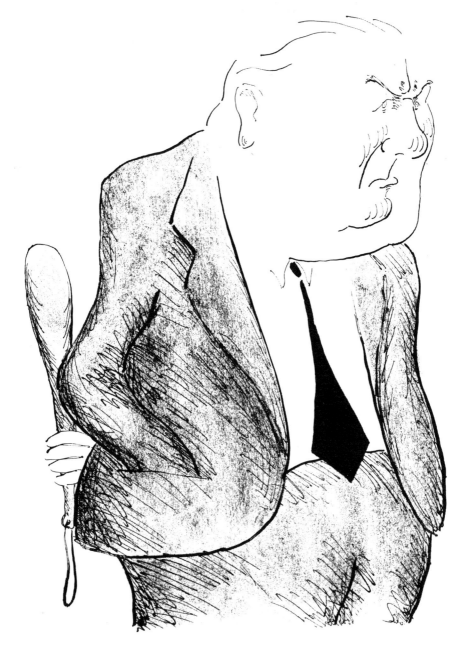

Jim's childish mouth curved upwards at the corners
And *Denis*'s curved downwards, like a mourner's.
The first to speak was *Jim*. He was the straight-man,
While *Denis* was the man-you-love-to-hate man.
'Phew. It's a big hello,'

                laughed *Jokin' Jim*,
'From me and it's a small hello from him.

He's looking pretty gloomy, isn't he?
Not me, though, 'cos I've got the *T.U.C.*
Behind me in the struggle all the way,
Just so's I more or less do what they say.
Not matter how acute the Situation
I'll go on with the fight for Moderation.'
By 'moderation' *Jim* meant curbing *Tittery*.
Excessive *Tittery* made *Wall Street* jittery,
And when that happened *Kissinger* turned catty,
And when *that* happened *Jokin' Jim* went batty,
Since finally what *Jokin' Jim* cared most about
Was having *Henry*'s warm regard to boast about—
Though *Kissinger* thought *Jim*'s opinions drivel
And barely even bothered to be civil.

'You've heard your Foreign Secretary's views,'
Said *Denis*.
                    'Now you must hear mine. Fair do's.
As anybody reasonable knows
We have to wake the country from its doze.
As Chancellor I must announce large cuts
In Social Services. The ifs and buts
I may go into at a later date,
But as for now, retrenchment just can't wait.
We have to back the makers, not the takers —
And if that fails we'll have to pray like *Quakers*.'
An instant uproar broke out on the Left,
Which judged such cutbacks tantamount to theft.
And certainly, *Britt* thought, between this speech
And *Hatbox*'s was not too great a breach —
The kinship between *Denis*'s tough stance
And *Margo*'s seemed a mite too close for chance.
Britt saw grown men fall flat and burst out crying,
Mown down by the foul insults that were flying.
Lord Brownale stormed the footlights in a fit,
Cried:
        'I resign!'
                    and fell into the pit,
Where noisily he lay wedged by his tum
For some time upside down in the bass drum.
On stage the cast rode round on the revolve
Resolving that the Conference should dissolve.
The Left was shouting promises to do them.
The Left ripped out the red plush seats and threw
                                                them,

While *Dismal Denis* vomited obscenities
About the injuries to the amenities.
The Left deplored the flagrant breach of trust.
The Left was in a frenzy of disgust.
Then why, *Britt* wondered, did not *Titt* and *Phutt*
Do more than stand about and say tut-tut?
This fearful racket was the Left's *non placet*,
So why did not those two Left-wingers back it?
Because someone, she realized with a qualm,

Had given them the order to stay calm.
Somewhere this whole performance had been planned!
Somewhere a genius was in command!
'This is a gun I'm holding,'

                    hissed a voice.
'You are to come with us. There is no choice.'
And with the argy-bargy at its height
Britt Bright was hauled away into the night.

BOOK NINE

PURSUED by pressmen's cabs and shrieking *Pandas*
The stolen car ran scattering bystanders
Through *Soho, Mayfair,* up and down *Park Lane*
And round in circles like a clockwork train.
It lurched through corners with its muffler dangling.
It bounced off buses with its hubcaps jangling.
The driver used a pistol-butt to break
A peep-hole when the windscreen turned opaque.
The howling gale assailed *Britt*'s eyes and ears
As unsuccessfully she fought back tears.
Britt's kidnappers were desperate to a man
And seemed to have but one coherent plan—
To find a sleeping house where they could hide
Or bargain with the lives of those inside.
Few *British* Left-wing groups are as *outré* as
The STROLLING REVOLUTIONARY PLAYERS,
And they, *Britt* realized, feeling Godforsaken,
Were these by whom she'd been so rudely taken—
Though for what reason she as yet knew not.
She recognized the wheelman as *Ken Trott,*
Producer of Committed TV series
Propounding undiluted *Marxist* theories.
Beside him *Kika Klutz* sat with a *Sten,*
A mortar, two bazookas and a *Bren.*
(I should say here that all these guns were toys:
The kind that when you crank them make a noise.
The players were outraged by the aspersion
Conversion to their faith required coercion.)
The hard-eyed heavy who had stuck *Britt* up
Was RAVEN REDRAG, spiteful as a pup.
He held his gun on her in the back seat,
Which left his famous sister free to bleat
Incessant slogans, tags, threats and demands—

To talk, VICTROLA REDRAG used both hands.
A peerless propagandist was *Victrola*,
Her brain pre-programmed like a pianola,
Her endlessly renewed circumlocution
Like *Trotsky*'s notion of a Revolution.
'The *Labour* Party is once more revealed,'
Victrola ranted as they rocked and reeled,
'Objectively as a repressive tool
Which (click) which helps the Capitalists rule.
The System now stands shorn of its disguise.
Our aim must (click) must be to Dramatize
The basic structure of our Consciousness
In terms the (click) the Workers can assess,
And (click) and (click) and (click) and (click) and thus
Provoke them to Examine and Discuss
The Mechanisms which (click) which (click) which
Are used to keep them servile by the Rich.
The *Labour* Party is once (click) once more ... '
And on she went exactly as before.
By now there was a honking, clanging fleet
Of cars in hot pursuit. From street to street
The fugitives fled twisting and flew turning
But all they left behind was rubber burning —
The posse kept on narrowing the gap
And closing in from all over the map
By truck, van, motorcycle, bike and tandem.
The time had come to seize a house at random.
They turned into a side street, hit the brakes
And picked a likely dwelling. In two shakes
The lock was blasted out and they were in.
'Now — let's speak frankly — what an awful din,'
Said HAROLD WILES,

                  'and, frankly, what a mess.
I'm not sure that you've got the right address.'
With mingled fear and awe the gang stood frozen,
Appalled it was *10 Downing Street* they'd chosen.
All unawares they'd mounted their invasion
To coincide with the august occasion
Of *Harold Wiles*'s Birthday. *Number 10*

Presented such a teeming scene my pen
Must sputter and give up before begun
The task of introducing one by one
The women of renown and men of parts
In every bailliwick from Sports to Arts
Who'd dressed up to the nines and by the cluster
Made haste to toast the host and lend their lustre.
Charles Charming, Prince of Wales, was there of course,
And *Princess Anne,* escorted by her horse.
My *Lady Freesia* stood keeping watch
On *Harold Half-Pint*'s progress through the scotch,
While *Lady Highrise* flowered at the side
Of proud *Wee Georgie* (soon to be *Lord*) *Wide.*
Huge Welshman, now *Sir Huge,* was in attendance,

Immensely pleased to have attained transcendence.
Urbane *Chief Clerk* was with LORD TEDDYBEAR,
And there *Lord Fatman* stood, and there and there.
And here *Lords Butchfield, Polaroid* and *Wiggle*
Were grouped around *Dick* (now *Sir Richard*) *Jiggle* ...
But I could make the list go on for years
Of these grand ladies and their cavaliers,
And barely get beyond the mere recital
Of those exalted with some kind of title —
When those without one who had graced the binge
Were of the calibre of *Dr Fringe,*
Russ Kennell, Harry Seaslug, Peter Balls ...
They jammed the joint until they cracked the walls,
And yet in all this glittering array
No doubt was possible of who held sway;
In all this vast cotillion of the Prominent
You couldn't miss the one man truly dominant;
The focus, fulcrum, bull's-eye, heart-beat, hub,
Pith, pivot, core, nerve, nucleus and nub
Of all this nexus, network, concentration,
Moot, meeting, mish-mash and conglomeration
Was *Harold Wiles, Prime Minister* of *Britain* —

Who now stood looking thoughtfully hard-bitten,
Assessing what he might do for the best
About the hardware pointed at his chest,
If 'chest' is not an epithet misplaced
For what occurred between his neck and waist.
To penetrate the soul of *Harold Wiles* —
A challenge past my skill by many miles.
To pin down the profound *M.P.* for *Huyton* —
One's cheeks can only whiten and throat tighten
At even contemplating such a task:
Wheels within wheels, and masks behind the mask!
Far, far beyond the ken of aeons previous
The character of *Harold Wiles* was Devious.
In practical affairs his grasp was tenuous
On any course except the disingenuous.
With his whole heart he looked upon mendacity
As preferable at all points to veracity
In keeping his great Party unified
Around himself as its perpetual guide —
An ageless and all-knowing tribal chief,
A *Moses* unencumbered by Belief,
Who would, in order to maintain his power,
Assert that hot was cold and sweet was sour,
Though ever and anon he'd change his tack
And after calling black white, call white black.
Prince of Deceit, he ruled without a rival —
Haroun El Half-Truth, Sultan of Survival,
Who from Antiquity and through Modernity
Had reigned supreme, and would until Eternity.
Or so, at any rate, it thus far seemed:
But who knew how, what, where and when he
                                        schemed?
Concerning *Wiles*, one fact was indisputable:
That he was orientally Inscrutable.
Through all manœuvrings, however massive,
The tiny eyes of *Wiles* remained impassive.
He fought his way through water and through fire
Equipped with pint of mild and faithful briar,
The jar held high and prop pipe kept ablaze

Whenever he was in the public gaze,
Though privately he liked cigars and brandy—
And woe to hosts who had not got them handy,
Lest *Wiles*'s world-renowned inscrutability
Be straightaway transformed into hostility.
Tonight, however, *Harold Wiles* the mummer
Was just as much at ease as when, each Summer,
In shorts and sandals, shin-bones looking chilly,
He played the fool around the *Isles* of *Scilly*.
For though *Wiles* looked paternally annoyed,
This was the kind of thing he most enjoyed:
He liked to find himself out on a limb
So long as all the limelight was on *him*.
The same way *Nurse Cavell* defied the *Huns*
Wiles stood there with his face towards the guns,
Flanked and surrounded by his entourage,
Who ranked in influence from small to large—
The voices at his ear composed a choir.
Joe Strange was there, and *Bernard Donforhire*,
And, even closer, *Lady Farkinell*,
Who held, some said, *Wiles* in a magic spell.
I've hardly time or space to name the rest—
But *Tommi Buda* stood with *Nikki Pest*,
A pair of *European* ethnic comics
Whose cross-talk act was based on Economics.
And there were *Gerald Mauffpiece* and — but *basta*.
Enough of the small fry. Back to their master,
Who stood, as I've been saying now for pages,
Four-square and steadfast like the Rock of Ages,
And lit his trusty pipe with nerveless hands
While fair *Victrola* spouted her Demands.
'We come,'
         she rapped,
                  'to set the Workers free
From you, the Bourgeois (click) the Bourgeoisie.'
At this, *Wiles* smiled a patronizing smile
Revealing a collage in modern style
Of quartz-crowned mandible and capped incisor
As false as *Don Quixote*'s pasteboard visor.

'Let's face the facts. You've come to the wrong man.
No, let me finish,'
                    Harold Wiles began.
'When you said that, of course I had to laugh.
The fact is that I'm just the Centre Half.
I don't do any more than lead the team
And keep our strike—our *forwards*—on the beam.
My place is in the middle of the park.
I'm *Jackie Charlton*. I've got men to mark.
If you want miracles done At A Stroke
You should have voted for that other bloke.
I'll just say frankly, fearlessly, that I—
And this, I think, nobody can deny—
That I have served a Government which cares.
That's what the Social Contract's for. Fair shares.
Paid out in decently agreed amounts
The Pound that's In Your Pocket is what counts,
Provided that it doesn't keep inflating—
Which means some people have to be kept waiting
And—no, I've started now, please let me finish—
And that's a fact I frankly don't diminish.
But on the whole—I've said this very often ... '
The tension eased. Hard hearts began to soften.
Among the Revolutionary group
The barrels of the guns began to droop.
The Radicals were slowly robbed of will
As if they had been running up a hill.
Eroded by that unrelenting mumble
Their castles in the air began to crumble.
Like Lotos-eaters fighting heavy eyes
They floated on a tide of Compromise,
A dream soft as a cloud, sweet as contrition ...
And so at last they swooned into submission,
The Flying Squad arriving to disarm them ·
As *Wiles* gave strict instructions not to harm them,
For though his notion of the way to keep
The peace was to send everyone to sleep,
It couldn't be denied the peace was kept—
For just so long as everybody slept.

(104)

BOOK TEN

THE last act. Every member of my cast
  Was on the scene or else approaching fast.
The noise of glasses clinking and corks popping
Grew deafening and went on without stopping.
The *Labour* chiefs arrived with much to-do.
The *Tory* Shadow Cabinet turned up too.
And now with eager cries the *Fleet Street* Editors
Came crowding in like *Casanova*'s creditors.
Around *Britannia Bright* they swarmed adoringly.
They snatched her to their chests and squeezed
                            imploringly,
Each offering the *Moon* for an Exclusive,
With protestations more and more effusive
Of marriage, wealth and similar delights
In payment for the Syndication Rights.
Red Menace! Mortal Danger! Flight to Glory!
Released Girl Kidnap Hostage Tells Own Story!
And now the *Beeb* and *I.T.N.* news crews
Came rolling in agog for interviews.
With giant lamps and little clip-on mikes
They strapped her down and got at her like shrikes,
Though PETER JAW made tentative suggestions
Which only slowly turned out to be questions.
'Miss *Bright*, now that you're sitting safe and sound,'
Said *Jaw*,
            'with friendly faces all around ...'
('At this point *Britt* was almost overcome.
She'd just seen *Midge* and *Heidi* in the scrum!
With all their differences, what friends they were,
Each to the other, both of them to her!
Britt sat and glowed with sisterly affection
While *Jaw* maintained his tone without deflection.)
Here in this house, the model of our State,

A house owned by no man, however great ...'
Britt's *Mum* and *Dad* were ushered into shot —
Examples of what being great was not.
'A house no wealth can buy nor greed can sell,
Where Change and Continuity both dwell ... '
The audience's eyes were all on *Britt*:
Sufficient cause for *Wiles* to have a fit.
It barely showed, of course. A nostril twitched.
Somewhere a jacket gusset came unstitched.
Wiles didn't need to scream or tear his hair
To indicate that he was going spare.
His close advisers watched him with alarm,
Afraid his pounding heart might do him harm.
By certain subtle signs they could well gauge
That *Wiles* was half incapable with rage.
The Press had once again conspired against him!
And people wondered why these men incensed him!
So thoroughly to have his thunder stolen —
It pained him like a poker up the colon,
Or pins applied to places I can't mention.
Somehow he had to win back their attention.
But what to do to get out of the fix?
He'd long ago used up all his old tricks.
The Press knew he'd do anything at all —
Swerve, swivel, dicker, dodge, connive and crawl —
So long as he could stay on at the top
And see the QUEEN on *Tuesdays* ... Hey, wait! Stop!
A new Idea! Its boldness made him gasp.
Yes, Immortality was in his grasp!
A Scheme not just to keep his lofty station
But to transcend it — through Renunciation!
Of all those called to drink deep from the cup
Who is more famed than him who gives it up?
Thenceforward what he was he always is,
What he feigned not to want forever his.
And yet ... Oh *God*, not yet ... So soon ... No,
                                        please ...

But this was it. The moment he must seize.
Loser takes nothing. *Wiles* made up his mind,

(106)

And pulled his greatest gamble. He resigned.

* * * * * * * * * * * *

I leave a line of asterisks to serve
In lieu of what, if said, might shake your nerve.
Some feelings go too deep to be portrayed,
Emotions too extreme to be displayed.
Though *Number 10* was full to overflowing
The crowd inside it somehow kept on growing,
A palpitant cross-section of the Nation
Which now was numb, bereft of all sensation
Except an overwhelming insecurity —
A panic of extraordinary purity.
You could have heard a pin drop as all eyes
Were switched from *Britt* to *Wiles* in hurt surprise,
The only sound a hiss of indrawn breath
As if all present felt the threat of Death.
They felt afraid. They felt as great a need
To follow as *Wiles* felt a need to lead.
They felt the end had come. They felt as trepid
As any flock of sheep without a shepherd.
They felt that this was more than they could bear.
They felt themselves to see if they were there.
They were. This was no nightmare. This was real!
They burst into a clamorous appeal
And every pleading word in the Thesaurus
They chanted like an ill-drilled Tragic Chorus.
The Best and Brightest grovelled on their knees.
Fine ladies had the vapours on settees.
Unhinged by terror, plagued with nameless fears,
Men ran amok, mascara ran with tears.
Forgotten, *Britt* surveyed the scene in wonder.
Was this new move by *Wiles* a thoughtless blunder,
Or just a way to fight another day —
A way of falling back *pour mieux sauter*?
The *French* phrase would be fitting, should his role
Turn out to echo that of *Charles de Gaulle*,
Who quit the field the better to return.
Yes, *Britt Bright* had at last begun to learn

(107)

That 'Politician' is a term denotive
Of one whose gift is to conceal the motive
For anything he does or does not do—
The only code to which he's always true.
Believing that in order to be ruled
The People must consistently be fooled,
The most he offers is to fool them fairly—
And even that much happens only rarely.
Whatever *Wiles*'s long-term plans, however
(And no one doubted *Wiles* was being clever),
His Ministers seemed not to be in doubt
That the Succession needed sorting out,
Since *Michael Phutt* was hopping on one boot
Attempting to put on a dark blue suit,
And *Dismal Denis* looked a bit reflective
Presumably regretting his invective,
And *Tony Wedgtail Titt* had squared his jaw
If possible more firmly than before
(You wondered how his teeth could stand the grind),
And *Junket* was pretending not to mind
That *Jokin' Jim* had suddenly extended
To all the Union Leaders he'd befriended
A warm grin, a glad handshake, a free fag
And licorice allsorts in a paper bag.
They clustered round him puffing smoke and chewing:
Jim looked as if he knew what he was doing.
But that's another story. One thing's certain—
It's time our cast of thousands took a curtain.
A reverent hush expunged the frightful din.
HER MAJESTY THE QUEEN came sweeping in,
And smiling the most satisfied of smiles
Created a new Knight: SIR HAROLD WILES.
With star and garter, *Gannex* cape and sash
And velvet hat he cut a splendid dash,
A blaze of glory soon obscured by fumes—
His pipe had set fire to his ostrich plumes.
The day was saved by *Lady Farkinell*,
Who snatching up a siphon rushed to quell
The conflagration with a gush of soda—

And MARY WILES supplied a brilliant coda,
Emerging with a blush from the dumb waiter
To make a Great Occasion even greater
By reading out her latest composition—
Reprinted here in full, by kind permission.

Amazement's Object, Peerless Patroness!
Methinks forsooth I durst presume to bless
Thy chaste munificence with jocund warble
For thus conferring such a precious bauble.
More joyfully no corncrake never carolled
Than I for pride in my dear husband *Harold*,
Who never will yield up, through sale or barter,
So beautiful a gift as thy sweet *Garter*.
Most Regal article of underclothing!
Denoting Love, the opposite of Loathing.
Great *Queen*! I could go on, but doubts assail me.
Alas, my fickle Muse has fled! Words fail me.

Forgetting for the nonce its agitation
The congregation roared in acclamation.
Lord Teddybear looked shyly at his toes
And sighed:
                'I taught her everything she knows.'
Sir Harold Wiles was on the point of tears
And all his pals he straightaway made peers.
As friends make plans and enemies make friends
In fond euphoria our story ends.
A *Corot* falls unnoticed off the wall
Responding to a tremor in *Whitehall*,
Where someone tries to bomb the *Cenotaph*.
Perhaps the bang shows on a seisomograph,

But at the party people dance and sing
And fool around and never hear a thing.
Is this complacency, or just confusion?
About that you must draw your own conclusion,
Since *Britt*, with *Midge* and *Heidi* her two chums,
Resolves henceforth to take Life as it comes,
As arm in arm they walk (this bit's pure corn)
Beside the pink *Mall* in the pearl-grey dawn.
Abandoned by the dissipating dark
The chill lies knee-deep in *St James's Park*:
The groomed grass drinks discreetly from the mist.
The solitude is an anaesthetist.
The streets are void. Of traffic, not a sound—
Except where round and round and round and round
The roundabout before the *Palace* gates
The *Liberal* Party taxi circulates
Approximately twenty times per minute—
But *Jerry Merry* is no longer in it.
Hyde Park. An equine snort. The smack of hooves.
Behind that screen of trees, what is it moves?
Are these the Phantom Horsemen come at last
At whose appearance all shall stand aghast?
Are these the ones whose riding-cloaks are shrouds,
Whose eyes are holes, whose high-road is the clouds?
Well no, not really. Nothing so portentous.
As yet no sure-fire token has been sent us.
We live in doubt. As *Britt* found out at length,
In that, perhaps, lies our remaining strength.
As long as we are not sure how to choose
It must mean we've got *something* left to lose—
And anyway, a certain-seeming sign
As soon could mean renewal as decline.
Though prophets of disaster have cast runes,
Read tea-leaves, studied entrails and bent spoons,
The CITY has lived through another night.
Good luck to it, and to *Britannia Bright*,
Whose *Diaries* I'm sure the world will hail
As leaving *Richard Crossman's* looking pale.
I understand the *Sunday Times* has planned

(111)

To get them banned to stimulate demand,
And as for those who haven't time to read—
The film's got *Barbra Streisand* in the lead.
The deal's still vague, but this much is specific:
As *Harold Wiles, Charles Bronson* should be terrific.

Britannia Bright's Bewilderment in the Wilderness of Westminster is the successor to *Peregrine Prykke's Pilgrimage* and *The Fate of Felicity Fark* – the two poems which have restored the comic epic both as an instrument of satire and as a source of entertainment. This time the subject at hand is Politics. The time-scale is the same: some time or any time in the last decade. The place is the same: London, the cockpit of a vanished Empire, where everything is in decay and transition. But the cast is very different. Instead of the literati and the media-men we are shown the politicians, from ex-luminaries like Lord Brownale and Sir Mac McHack to the people who actually control our destinies: Jokin' Jim and Dismal Denis, Tony Wedgtail Titt, and Shirley Whirley. Here are Ted Tede and Margo Hatbox, Enoch Eunuch and Clive Perkins. And looming above them all, infinitely subtle, is the figure of the master manipulator, Harold Wiles. What does his resignation actually mean?

This is only one of the questions asked by Britannia Bright, who, as her name suggests, represents the gifted youth of a nation – a nation at the crossroads. Her poem, though even funnier than its predecessors, marks a new seriousness in its author, Clive James. And the drawings, by Marc, set standards of pitiless inquiry unapproached even by his much-lauded illustrations for *Felicity Fark*.

£1.95 net
IN UK ONLY

ISBN 0 224 01309 X